CHANGE MANAGEMENT
- JUST DOING IT!

For a complete list of Management Books 2000 titles,

visit our web-site on http://www.mb2000.com

CHANGE MANAGEMENT - JUST DOING IT!

Robert L Sullivan
and
Stephen Lytton

2000

First published in 2000 by Management Books 2000 Ltd
Cowcombe House
Cowcombe Hill
Chalford
Gloucestershire GL6 8HP
Tel. 01285 760 722
Fax. 01285 760 708
E-mail: mb2000@compuserve.com

Printed and bound in Great Britain by Biddles, Guildford

British Library Cataloguing in Publication Data is available
ISBN 1-85252-351-4

Contents

Acknowledgements

This book tells a story in which many people played parts, some small, some large. I was privileged to be both one of the characters in the story and an observer of the roles others played as the plot unfolded. Now, as chronicler of the events, I remain only one small part of a greater effort. I should like therefore to express my sincere appreciation to all the following people for their contribution either to the transformation process of Sellotape, which forms the basis of the book, or for their contribution to getting the book published. To all these people, I offer my heartfelt thanks.

Franck Ullmann and Rory Cullinan gave me a unique opportunity to learn and experiment with managing change programmes in their business, and they continued to back my somewhat adventurous ideas throughout the journey of discovery in Sellotape. Without their having taken the considerable risk that they did, there would have been no story to write, and many of us who worked in Sellotape would have been lesser individuals than we are today.

This book details only a few of the thousands of success stories; many of them small in size but large in both their cumulative effect and impact. It was the men and women who worked with me in Sellotape who accomplished these successes. Although some names are mentioned in the book, where this helps to bring the story to life, there are many more unsung heroes out there whose efforts warrant just as much recognition. Furthermore, there will certainly be hundreds of inspiring stories detailing successes, failures, frustrations and satisfaction, which, had I heard of them, I may have mentioned. I wish to thank every one of those fine people for helping turn my dreams and ideas into reality. This is their story.

Amongst all my colleagues, I want especially to acknowledge the support of my management teams in leading the change programmes – the members of the Operations Management team in Sellotape GB and the Sellotape Industrial Senior Management Team: Richard Bower, Phil Bray, Ray Funnell, Ian McGillivray, Simon Hayes,

Andrew Houston, Peter Jones, Dieter Pfaff, Harald Spönagel, Ian Stringer, Richard Symes, Jacques Tencé, Richard Wood, and Lionel Wortley.

And, finally, I should like to acknowledge the contribution made by Steve Lytton, my co-author and Network Co-ordinator of CLASP (Central Logistics Association for Supply-chain Partnerships) in Bedfordshire and North Buckinghamshire, without whom the Sellotape story would never have been written. It was Steve who, in the very early days of my time with Sellotape, recognised that some of the work we were doing was worthy of sharing with others; and so started a series of presentations about what we were doing to other people interested in managing change. The interest in our experiences grew to a point where I thought that there might be some merit in committing some of them to paper. I first went to Steve with a vague idea about writing a book, because I knew he had been involved in publishing. Our association quickly developed into a partnership in which Steve converted my rather clinical narrative of events into something which is a pleasure to read, while at the same time extracting the human story lurking behind every management process or action.

If any manager or chief executive is, in some small way, better able to lead and manage change as a result of reading about our experiences, then both Steve and I will have achieved our objective in writing this book

Robert Sullivan
24 April 2000

Introduction

Change is big business! The shelves of every bookshop groan under the weight of volumes expounding the latest theories of change management. People make fortunes writing about their insight into what we should do: invert the organisation, develop a matrix or even allow natural organic order to evolve out of the chaos. There are change management seminars galore and we are invited to listen in awe to the wisdom of this or that guru of the new management science. Theories abound, usually denoted by some or other three-letter acronym, which, we are told, we ignore at our peril. And, for fear of being caught without 'a programme', we mere mortal managers tend to grab hold of a passing theory and attempt to apply it in our business. Sometimes this succeeds. More often than not, the results are downright useless, if not unpleasant, and we have to latch on to the next wizard offering to get us out of the mess.

If you are hoping that this book will provide a new theory of change management, a new acronym, or the management equivalent of Stephen Hawking's 'theory of everything', you are about to be disappointed. I recommend that you either buy it as a doorstop or place it strategically on an office shelf, to indicate to others that you read a lot about management. What I would not do, however, is pass it on to the competition, because what it does contain is a set of practical lessons from someone who has led organisational change from the sharp end. It is a book about making change happen in practice on the factory floor and in the office. It is an account of sizing up the challenge of change and then just doing it.

To some, however, the lessons of the past might appear to be somewhat 'old hat'. After all, most of my experience pre-dates e-business, and so might seem scarcely relevant to today's world. It is certainly true that, at the time that I am writing this book, e-business is becoming ever more influential in terms of the business environment. But this exactly illustrates the point. As these and other new challenges continue to beset organisations, managers are going to find themselves increasingly needing to effect change successfully, bringing their people on board in the process. The lessons learnt from change programmes in the 1990s will be just as relevant in the twenty-first century. In fact, the demand for change management expertise will be greater than ever.

Most people in business take it for granted that change is a necessity for survival. Globalisation and the Internet age have meant that the environment in which we live and do business is changing at an unprecedented rate. As technology has advanced and business efficiency grown, mankind has become hooked on the idea of an ever-increasing standard of living. Demands continue to increase and further twists are added to the spiral of radical change. What was good enough for yesterday is not good enough for today, let alone tomorrow. The writing is on the wall for any manager who still clings to the belief that he does not need to change.

But, to be a success in management, you don't have to be a business school graduate. I didn't read a management book until 1991, believing that they were just for consultants and not for real managers. Having trained as a scientist, I cut my teeth in business in South Africa, where life is rough and ready, and one succeeds by getting things done. Being caught reading a management book might leave one open to the accusation of being an academic rather than a real manager. Now, having spent some 25 years of my life in manufacturing, across a whole array of industries from beer brewing to sticky-tape, and having a collection of works by suitably impressive authors, I still have the tendency to resort to my own experience and capabilities when facing an organisational problem. Perhaps it's just the challenge of developing unique solutions to problems. However, all too often I find that I have ploughed a lot of time and energy into thinking up a way of resolving an issue, only to discover that someone else has solved a similar problem and then written a book about it. I really should read more of those tomes!

I started my career as a junior manager by taking on the management of the fermentation department in a brewery whose 'competitive edge' was that it was unable to make beer that was not contaminated in some way or other! I got to work and we soon turned the operation into an efficient and well-run plant. And what it a buzz it was! Indeed, I got so addicted to this buzz that I have spent the rest of my life seeking out troubled organisations that I could help fix. As time went by, the organisations got larger and the responsibilities broader until I was taking on major business turn-around and culture change programmes in the role of managing director. Thus, I have had 25 years of fixing companies, a quarter of a century of managing change.

This book relates some of my experiences with the Sellotape International Group, first in leading a culture change programme within one function, and then in the design and implementation of a new organisation for the industrial business. It details some of the obstacles, processes, key drivers and measures that we encountered and used in achieving a successful result. This is, of course, all hindsight. In reality, at the time, we usually knew what we wanted to achieve, but little more. Mostly we made up solutions as we went along. Sometimes we got it right and sometimes not. When we found we were not getting the outcome we wanted, we went back and tried something different, until we eventually got it right. In so doing, we learnt some very valuable lessons which I hope will be useful to other managers out there – ordinary people like myself who are struggling to carry out the changes in their organisations that will make the difference between survival and obscurity.

I hope that others will be able to draw on these experiences and thus avoid having to go through the same discovery process that I did. With this in mind, I have attempted to summarise what we did in management process terms at the end of each chapter as simply as I can. I hope that this will help pragmatists like myself to extract the lessons from this book quickly and easily without having to read the whole thing. Those with a little more of an academic bent or with more time on their hands will, I hope, enjoy reading about the experiences and will no doubt draw their own conclusions from the text. There is perhaps more to learn from my mistakes and omissions than there is from the achievements. But that, I would suggest, is the nature of change management.

Part 1

Culture Change

1

Setting up the Organisation

Amongst all the other the job adverts, this particular one stood out as somewhat special. For a start, the layout was good, but it was what the text left out that interested me. I read it through again and still couldn't identify the company. But the post was for an Operations Director and, being on the lookout for a new challenge at the time, I thought I'd give it a shot.

The usual trail of interviews followed and, soon enough, the recruitment consultant let me know that I was very highly placed on the shortlist. There remained just one more hurdle to jump – a meeting with the Group Chief Executive, Franck Ullmann. His would be the final decision and I was scheduled to meet him for breakfast at Browns Hotel in West London a few days later. My mind conjured up a picture of a greying gentleman in a Saville Row suit. After all, that is what Chief Executives look like, don't they?

So, on the appointed day, still armed with my personal array of prejudices, I set to the task of gearing myself up to the deal with this elder statesman.

I arrived at Browns as arranged and asked for Mr Ullmann at the Reception Desk. No luck. He wasn't in his suite, but the clerk suggested I try the breakfast room. I did, but there wasn't a grey hair to be seen. I hung around for a few minutes, trying, but failing, I suppose, to look nonchalant. Then, suddenly, a swarthy young man wearing a blue shirt with half-rolled-up sleeves, a skewed tie, and a pair of light coloured trousers appeared from the breakfast room. "Ah, Mr Ullmann," said the receptionist, "your visitor is here." I could feel my eyes darting around in their sockets. And then my face broke into a smile as I returned the warm and friendly grin that confronted me. "What have we here?" I said to myself.

While I tackled a plate of bacon and eggs, Franck – a Frenchman, as it transpired – dunked a croissant in his coffee and smoked several Gauloises. His manner of explanation was brief and to the point, and, behind the cigarette fug and the somewhat manic gestures and unconventional behaviour, I could clearly detect a lightening mind and a true sense of purpose. I felt sure that, if there was one person I could work with, it was Franck Ullmann.

It seemed that Franck and his partners had bought the Sellotape Group a year or so earlier. The company had been in decline and some harsh decisions had been taken to stop the rot. One of the four factories had been closed, costs had been cut and the UK operation had crept back into the black – but only just. "The culture in the factory is wrong. We have to change it," said Franck. "We are looking for an Operations Director who will take on the task."

As Franck had outlined the situation, I knew the job represented a considerable challenge, but, for some reason I have never totally understood, I was inspired by this rather unusual Frenchman with a sparkle in his eye and a burning mission to rescue his organisation. Franck offered me the position, and I accepted. Had he been the kind of grey-haired elder statesman I had expected, I would probably have turned him down. After all, it meant leaving a secure job with a very successful pharmaceutical multinational for a relatively small business struggling to survive. However, at times one needs that extra special voltage burst to smash through the boundaries of complacency and inertia. Working with Franck promised just that.

At the time, Sellotape GB was a £40m company, making up about half the turnover of the whole Group. The Sellotape brand is a household name, but in fact the company's product range was far more extensive than just the clear sticky tape we use to wrap up Christmas presents. In all, there were four basic product categories:

- **Consumer Products** – a range of tapes used in the office and home, sold as standard individual units.

- **Adhesive Foams** – foam tapes of various thickness, density and adhesive character, used mainly in industry. Much of this is tailored to specific customer requirements, both in terms of the dimensions and the basic formulation of the foam and the adhesive. It is the kind of stuff used to stick mirrors to walls or to seal draughts around doorframes.

- **Technical Tapes** – similar to ordinary sticky tape in many respects, but developed for high-tech and industrial applications such as lithographic masking, high-temperature applications and electrical insulation. The difference lies in the nature of the film used and the adhesive applied.

- **Butyl** – black, sticky goo, which is extruded into strips with very precise profiles, sometimes combined with other materials such as films. It is used widely in the building industry, in such familiar applications as sticky flashing tape for sealing joints between roofs and walls.

The Company made tape by running a large roll of film through a coater, which applied the adhesive to the surface of the film, forming a 'Jumbo' – a large reel about one and a half metres wide and half a meter in diameter. Each Jumbo would be converted into the familiar small rolls by unwinding the film through a slitting machine and rewinding the narrow strips onto small cores. Foam tapes are produced in a similar manner, but with a foam sheet (also manufactured by Sellotape) replacing the film. On paper, it all sounds so simple. In reality, it was a very complex operation with thousands of different product varieties, and it was all in a state of confusion.

I eventually joined the company in September 1993. After the usual formalities, we got down to the real issue.

"The culture in Operations is wrong," said Franck, without beating about the bush. "I want you to change it."

I sat back to hear a few details of just what he was expecting. But nothing came. That was it – all the guidelines he was going to give. He didn't say what he wanted the culture changed *to*. He just made it plain that what he had was not what he wanted. I had a blank sheet of paper and a golden opportunity.

In the past, I had been part of a team that had been tasked with organisational change. During the SmithKline Beecham culture change programme that followed the merger of the two pharmaceutical giants, I had been in the thick of things along with others. It had been an experience that had thoroughly boosted my interest in change management in general. This time, however, it was going to be different. I would have total responsibility for the full change programme myself. I relished the prospect, but nevertheless felt a certain apprehension.

So, what were the key elements of Sellotape's culture that Franck perceived as being 'wrong'? They were just the sort one would expect to find in a long-established organisation that had been in decline over a long period, and which had been subjected to a number of rounds of vicious cost cutting. The managers were steeped in doing things the traditional way. Modern management practices, if known, were noticeable by their absence.

There was a sharp divide between management and the shop floor, with managers seeing their role as making decisions and that of the shop floor as being simply to do as they were told. For their part, shop-floor workers did not see decision-making as part of their job. After all, they weren't paid to make decisions, were they? The factory ran on a reactive basis, fire-fighting one crisis after another. As for forecasting of demand and planning, these were virtually non-existent. Where plans were actually written down, it was a miracle if anyone adhered to any of the details. One of the managers at the time described Sellotape as a 'hot business', meaning that there was no room for planning. The skill lay in being good at reacting to whatever came up. Thus, Production was expected to respond to every whim of the Sales Department, regardless of the cost or the disruption this caused. Naturally, meeting one panic order usually made twenty other orders late and led to a further twenty crises.

As regards the plant itself, the outward signs of confusion and lack of control were everywhere. Housekeeping was appalling and the factory floor was cluttered with work in progress. The customer service levels were dreadful, waste levels were high (where they were indeed measured) and a glance in the rubbish skip revealed that the logistics and cost of waste disposal was a real issue in itself. And what of the people in the business? Everyone was desperately trying to look after his own little bit, in order to ensure his or her own survival. There were a lot of very frustrated, weary and disillusioned people around.

Amongst the workforce were some genuine 'heroes' – those management relied on to get orders out when customers lost their sense of humour. However, the cost of this panic management had never been calculated, nor was there any structure in place capable of avoiding the same panic being repeated time and again. Franck's assessment had been spot on. If the company was to survive, Operations needed a new culture, and a vibrant, dynamic one at that!

From the outset, it was clear that, before we could get a culture change programme under way, I would need to assess the basic structure of the organisation to see if it was appropriate to meet the task of producing goods and actually getting them to the customer. This step would be fundamental. If it was a structural issue that lay behind Sellotape's inability to keep customers happy, then fire fighting would always remain the order of the day, and there would be no point whatsoever in addressing the question of the culture.

I began by looking at the factory from the customer and market end to identify the breaks in the supply line and discovered, with little surprise, that the way the factory was organised took no account of the supply line to the customer. (Fig. 1.1)

The Dunstable site layout was most unfortunate. It was split between two buildings, separated by a distance of some hundreds of yards. One of the buildings, known as Unit 15, housed a number of coaters, including three that produced foam products in Jumbo form. These were then converted into final products in the same building. A fourth coater in Unit 15 produced Jumbos of clear tape for the consumer market, which were then transported up the road to the second building, Unit 11. This unit housed the warehouse, and the conversion and packaging plant used to convert the products into their final form for the consumer market. Each unit had a separate manager, which meant that products destined for the consumer market had to pass from one building to another, as well as moving through two areas of responsibility on their journey through manufacture. If this wasn't problematic enough, the coating speed of a clear film runs at about 300m per minute, using hot melt adhesives, while foam manufacture and coating runs at about 10m per minute and requires significant drying and curing time for the adhesives. With such diverse technologies requiring different operational skills, it was clear that

19

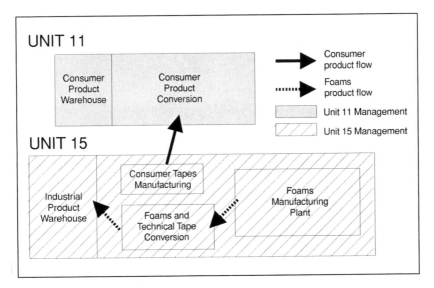

Fig 1.1 - The layout of the Dunstable factories and rthe organisation

having the same people attempting to do both jobs was destined to create difficulties.

Part of the problem lay in the fact that the chaps who produced the consumer Jumbos saw their job as having been completed when the Jumbo was sent to Unit 11. If any problem occurred with the product, they simply turned a blind eye and sent it up the road. The issue was brought home to me very graphically when I was walking around the plant a couple of days after starting at Sellotape. One of the operators on the consumer coating machine called me over.

"Hey, look at this," he said, pointing indignantly at a Jumbo. "Them up at Unit 11 have sent this Jumbo back here because they say they can't use it. Something about the roll having creases in it. What the heck do they think I can do about it?" The irony of the situation was lost on him. It was he who had made the product in the first place, but, because he had passed it on to 'them up the road', in his mind it was no longer his concern. He had passed it on and it was up to them to solve any subsequent problems.

The question of not seeing the next person down the line as one's customer was evidently a key issue to be tackled.

Another problem area lay in that all the service functions – engineering, quality and purchasing – were centralised. This meant that the production managers had no direct access to the services they needed to run their plants. Nor did those working in these functions identify with the overall purpose of the enterprise. An engineer, for example, saw his job as one of fixing machines when they broke down. He did not see himself as part of a team keeping the machines running in order to keep the customer happy. (Fig 1.2)

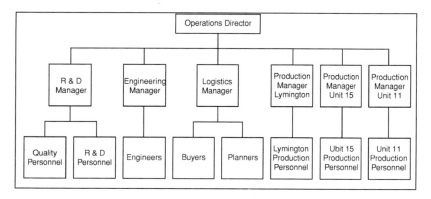

Fig 1.2 - The geographically based organisation

It was clear that the organisation and the responsibilities had to be changed. The ideal solution would have been to consolidate all the activities into one building, and create one management team. But this was not possible. Neither of the sites could accommodate all the plant and, given the poor profitability, there was no chance that funds would be forthcoming for a move to a new site that was big enough.

The solution was to organise production along product and market lines, and ignore the geography. All the plant involved in making products for the consumer market was put under the control of one production manager, while the plant for making foams became the responsibility of a second production manager. The conversion of technical tapes for the industrial market was included in the Foams Production portfolio. (Fig 1.3)

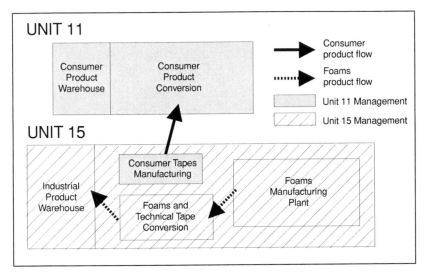

Fig 1.3 - The revised organisational responsibilitiy for the Dunstable factory units

Staff were allocated to Foams, Consumer, or Butyl Production, depending on which product they made, rather than the building in which they worked. This served to group together appropriate skills, machines and products. We also divided the service functions between the two production departments, giving each production manager a team of engineers, a buyer, and a quality team to support him.

Creating these teams around the supply chain rather than the geography had a number of significant advantages:

- It encouraged teamwork across the functions and disciplines.

- Expertise developed around the technologies associated with the product and market.

- The different dynamics of the markets could be addressed (typically the consumer market worked on a three-day lead time, and promotions were a regular feature. The industrial market, into which foams and technical tapes were sold, worked to lead times measured in weeks, and there was a very high proportion of made-to-order products).

22

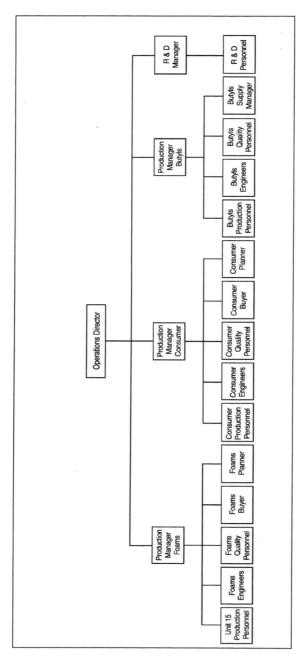

Fig 1.4 - The product and market-based organisation

The basic principle of the new organisation was put in place quickly, but allocating service functions to the individual production units had to be done in a number of stages, with some people initially remaining in a 'central' team servicing both units.

Now that the structure was right, the next critical matter was consolidating the management skills. As in most 'traditional' companies, the managers had grown up from within. Technical skills abounded, but these were not the skills required for the new culture – one that would make Sellotape into a World-Class company. The question was which of the managers would be able to adapt to new ways of working and be prepared to learn new skills.

This issue brought me into working closely with Rory Cullinan, the CFO and Franck's partner. Although I did not realise it at the time, he was to become my mentor for many years to come. Rory is a Scot for whom mumbling is the preferred mode of communication. That said, despite his misguided tendency to see people purely as a cost to be reduced whenever possible, he is probably the smartest businessman I have ever worked with. What with him and Franck, I really was in bed with a formidable pair and I was loving it.

I had been encouraged by my MD and fellow directors at the time to try to help the existing staff members develop into their new roles and, although I knew it would be difficult and time consuming, I did my best. Indeed, some of the managers quickly proved their ability to shift up a gear. However, some simply lacked the experience or the natural ability to drive through the changes we needed. Progress was slow.

Then, one Friday, some months after I had joined Sellotape, Franck made one of his regular flying visits to the UK. He called me into his office. Uh, oh! I thought as I sat down. It was not an experience I look back at with any joy. Franck was sitting there, grim-faced.

"I've just been in the warehouse," he said. "It's just not happening fast enough!" He was right. The poor housekeeping and the obvious inefficiencies had convinced him that the manager in charge of logistics was not up to the job. It was true; the manager concerned was indeed the weakest member of my team, having been promoted by my predecessor from a relatively junior clerical post to 'give him a chance'. Franck encouraged me to replace him. "We cannot afford the time to train people who are not up to the job," he said.

Over the weekend, I spent some time reflecting on the problems I had with the management team. Some managers were performing well, but others were clearly not able to deliver the changes we needed in order to survive. I had to take the bull by the horns and get the right people into all the critical functions.

On the Monday, I met Franck and Rory and put forward a plan to recruit four managers – three as replacements for existing positions and the fourth, a new post, with the title of 'Quality and Performance Development Manager'. To this day, I cringe at the thought of the title, but it was the best I could think of at the time. What we needed was someone who would facilitate change through training, and by adopting a systematic approach to resolving problems. Since the job would carry few routine management duties, the first thing I needed this person to think about every morning was "What do I need to do today to improve the performance of this organisation?". The 'Quality' bit of the title identified the manager's responsibility for revitalising the Company's quality systems, which, instead of being a dynamic engine for growth, had simply become administrative activities designed to keep the ISO 9000 auditor off our backs.

In seeking to recruit the new managers, we used a very reputable consultant. The jobs would be tough and so we hiked up the salaries in order to attract high quality applicants, and advertised anonymously. Here I committed a serious error. I'm sure you know how it is: you don't want to cause upset ... but, naturally, within days, it was clear to anyone working at Sellotape that certain posts were about to become vacant and, even though we had told those who were being replaced about their fate before the advertisement was placed, a whole set of feathers were seriously ruffled. This was all the more so since we hadn't indicated publicly that we were intending to change the management structure or the salary levels. This episode taught me never to try recruiting clandestinely. You almost always get found out. It is much better to be open about your plans and intentions, and deal with the effects up front. It does not make it any easier, but it does at least reduce suspicion and mistrust.

Painful though it all was, we nevertheless succeeded in recruiting a group of very capable people from this exercise. Together with the older hands, we created a top-class team to tackle the problems and deliver the required changes. This team, with only one exception, was to remain the driving force throughout the next three years.

Management Stuff

The Approach

Organisational structure should always reflect an organisation's objectives. For business success, the structure should be designed to correspond to the customers' perspective and to satisfy their requirements. Management issues that this raises should be viewed as secondary problems to be resolved.

- Once the optimum structure has been devised, the fundamental building blocks must be put in place swiftly.

- New management should be brought in where necessary to bring new thinking, facilitate change and create a critical mass of skills. The nettle of unsuitable managers should be grasped early in the process, with those unwilling or unable to change being replaced.

Process

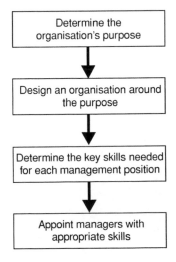

Fig 1.5 - The process

Key Points

- When introducing a culture change programme, buy-in from the top is essential.

- Ensure that you have capable managers in place swiftly.

- Be open and honest about what you are planning to do as early as possible. There will always be a price to pay in terms of emotion and disturbance, but the earlier this is tackled, the lower the total cost to the organisation.

- Clandestine recruitment will almost inevitably be discovered and will lead to mistrust in the future.

- Do not compromise on the calibre of the management you appoint and expect to pay the going rate to get them. An investment in good managers will always pay off.

2

Developing the Vision

Knowing something is wrong is one thing. Being able to effect the right kind of change is something else. Such was the problem that we faced. Where we were was not where we had to be. But then again, nobody knew exactly where we ought to be. It was quite a problem.

The first task, therefore, was to find a way of describing the kind of culture we needed to have, if we hoped for any long-term future for the business. Sure, we were all familiar with mission statements, strategies and value statements – after all, these had been in use in large businesses for years. But we shied away from using these particular terms, because they all sounded rather like packaged remedies for corporate ailments. What we wanted was a formula for Sellotape that encapsulated a mental picture of the Company as it would appear in the future – something simple that people could understand and relate to.

We came up with the term 'The Operations Vision'. This was to be a set of words describing what we were aiming to become, while also embodying the way we sought to behave and the way that we wished to be seen, both by those inside the organisation and by the outside world. Of necessity, it would have to be somewhat vague in nature at first, as it was describing something that we did not fully comprehend at the time. However, we knew, that as the process continued and we started to near the goal, the Vision would probably need to change to reflect the increased clarity.

We saw the Vision as being like the top of a mountain hidden by cloud. (Fig. 2.1) You know it is there; you have an idea of what it probably looks like, but all the details are obscured. Vague though this was, we considered this mental picture of the mountain top very useful. After all, if you are intending to climb a mountain, it is better

Without a Vision   **With a Vision**

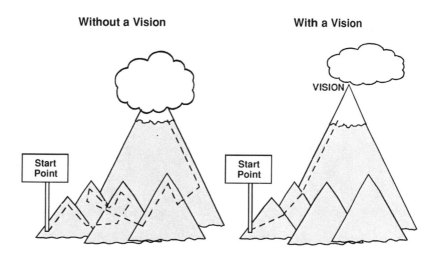

Fig 2.1 - The 'top-of-the-mountaion' vision analogy

to ignore the foothills that don't lead to the top and concentrate on those that do. It saves time, energy and wasted effort. For us, the Vision was to fill a similar role. Knowing roughly where we wanted to go would help us avoid doing things that would not help us get there. Anyway, the alternative – blindly crashing around hoping that we would create something we liked – was a prospect we neither relished, nor one that we had the luxury to employ.

What everyone in the organisation needed was a Vision of a new and better working environment. Morale was at virtually rock bottom. People had no clear purpose in their daily work, other than that of getting the job done and surviving to fight another day. It was hardly an atmosphere calculated to encourage enthusiasm, commitment, innovation, or the kind of momentum that would take the company forward.

Relief came in the guise of Performance Development Manager, Richard Symes. Richard introduced his Wedges and Magnets model to explain the purpose of a Vision in a culture change programme. (Fig 2.2) We were to refer to it many times over the next few years.

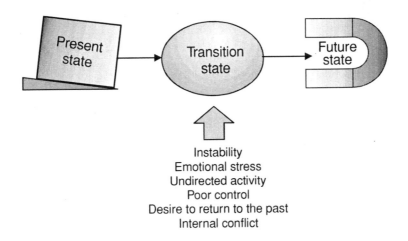

Instability
Emotional stress
Undirected activity
Poor control
Desire to return to the past
Internal conflict

Fig 2.2 - The 'Wedges and Magnets' model of change[1]

The basis of the model is that organisational change is a process, not an event. It can be summarised as follows:

- An event or a crisis disturbs a stable organisation. (Think of it as a wedge being driven under a block to destabilise it.)

- In this destabilised state, confusion begins to reign within the organisation, leaving people unsure of how to respond to the new situation. People start to react in ways that prove to be counter-productive. Much effort is wasted and morale begins to sink. Not having a Vision of a better future, people try to recreate what existed before the crisis, when life was much more comfortable.

- What is then required is a new Vision, depicting a future that is more attractive than the past – a magnet which draws people away from the past and away from the destabilised state, towards the new.

---

[1] This model is based upon one described by Daryl R Connor in *Managing at the Speed of Change* (John Wiley and Sons, 1998) pp 86-98. This in turn has its origins in *Readings in Social Psychology* by Kurt Lewin, ed EE Maccoby, TM Newcombe and EL Hartley (Holt, Reinhart and Winston, 1958, New York).

This model suited the experience of Sellotape perfectly. The company had had several wedges driven into it: a factory closure, substantial redundancies, changes in performance expectations, the introduction of flexible working and changes to senior management, to name just a few. The organisation was certainly unstable, and we needed a 'magnet' to mobilise it, to help it move out of its miserable state.

So far so good. The matter at issue was that, although Franck and Rory had effectively given me carte blanche in designing the culture of the future, I needed to be certain that what I was going to create would indeed correspond to their wishes. I needed to be 100% convinced that I had their total backing for the programme I was about to embark upon. Inevitably, the process was not going to be smooth and I needed to know that the chaps with the chequebook would be committed to what we were creating, despite any short-term pain they might have to endure. After some six weeks in the job, I had a firm idea of what was wrong in the business and what was needed for it to succeed.

I presented Franck and Rory with a SWOT analysis, and my Vision of the sort of organisation I wanted to create. (Fig 2.3)

To my great relief, they gave it the thumbs up. It had obviously struck a chord with Franck's underlying, if unspoken, thoughts.

Now, with my sponsors firmly behind me, I had to secure the buy-in and commitment of my management team. Experience had taught me that the team would not respond just because the bosses had endorsed my Vision. And, besides, I knew that the kind of organisation we needed to create demanded that the managers themselves develop a Vision that they considered their own. My view was that, as long as there was an overall coherence between the direction and spirit that my sponsors had signed up for and the Vision devised by the management team, Franck and Rory would support it. I showed the team what I had presented to our owners and then put it away in my drawer, never to be seen again. It was time to start working on OUR Vision.

Several of the managers in the team had spent most of their careers in the tapes business, which was of course a plus in many ways. However, the down side was that this experience had engendered a 'mind-set' – a paradigm – which tended to limit their appreciation of what might be possible in our business.

Cost:	Service:
• Low cost provider of high value product • Low inventory levels • Material cost in absolute decline • Ongoing productivity improvement • Waste halved every three years	• Focused on customers • Integrated planning systems • Supply chain managed from supplier to customer • Customer driven lead times • 99% customer service performance • Imaginative new products • High speed to market
Continuous improvement:	**People and Organisation:**
• Measures to drive improvement • Cross functional project teams • Problem definition and solving skills • Process based improvement • Use of external research • Outward looking	• Product and customer focused organisation • 3 management layers • Skilled in management and technology • Self-directed work groups • Multi-skilled work force • High motivation
Plant and processes:	**Quality:**
• Facility which impresses customers • Flexible plant and process • Low labour intensity • Pull-through material flow • High utilisation, high efficiency • Leading edge processes	• Ownership on shop floor • On-line measurement and control • Right first time culture • Design for manufacture and use • Defect rate halving every three years

Fig 2.3 - The first draft Operations Vision

The best way to open minds, we reckoned, was to visit other enterprises, to see first hand what others did and how they did it. It was a revelation! We visited a range of industries, from a dye manufacturer to a car fuel cap cover producer. We spend a day with one of our film suppliers, who had undergone a change programme of their own, when they had been on the brink of collapse. We watched videos describing business transformations and read articles about new management styles and practices. It was a true eye-opener. As we saw and experienced different management approaches and styles, and learnt how the people in the businesses responded to the new ways in which they were managed, it became clear to us all how businesses could achieve the apparently impossible.

The effect on the whole team was electric. After all, if all those other buggers could do it, why couldn't we? We now needed to move onto Stage Two – to devise our own Vision.

Soon we were off to a rather scruffy hotel in Oxfordshire for two days to get the ball rolling. This 'away period' had a dual purpose: to detail and formalise the Vision, and to get our team working more effectively. It was a masterstroke. The mere fact of getting away from the office for a few days immediately started to build the team spirit. But besides drinking lots of beer (which always tends to help more than a little), we also included some more structured activities to cement the team together.

Among these were some simple but challenging games that required the team to work together, as well as some straightforward tools that assessed the basic behavioural preferences of each individual in a team situation.

One of these, a questionnaire based instrument called 'Strength Deployment Inventory', was particularly useful. It was quick and simple, taking barely half an hour to complete and analyse. The results were easy to interpret and, at the end of the exercise, the team had a new appreciation of everyone's attributes. Things were starting to gel.

With the team dynamics operating well, we needed to get to work on developing our Vision and it was at this stage that I drafted in an outsider to facilitate the process. I felt that if we were to get to the heart of the matter, it would be essential that individuals felt free to express their hopes and desires without fear of any consequences whatsoever. John Taylor, from Octave Consulting, an old friend and associate of mine, took over the facilitation role with a free hand to do whatever was needed. It is true that I briefed him as to the general outline of the Vision I had agreed with Franck and Rory, but this was merely to give him some overall idea of the lie of the land.

Our first task was to agree on a set of headings for our Vision, and then to come up with some words under each heading to describe what we had in mind. It was exhausting and took nearly all of the two days. Every single word was examined, debated and discussed until we all understood and agreed what it meant. Laborious it might have been, but it ensured that we all came out the other end with a common understanding of what we had written down.

There was no confusion. Our words meant the same for each one of us. We had all been party to the process. The words were ours and we were proud of them. We had described the organisation we all wanted to create.

All fired up by the process, but knowing how difficult it can be to remember words, we felt we wanted some kind of visual portrayal of our Vision. Just as a three-pointed star in a circle immediately makes us think of Mercedes Benz, with all that this implies, we wanted a symbol (a metaphor, as I later came to know it) that would bring back all the memories, emotions and mental pictures that we shared.

The Vision was built around seven elements:

- Continuous Improvement
  - Customers
    - People
      - Performance
        - Quality
          - Systems
            - Technology

Finding a metaphor, however, turned out to be far from easy. We played around with endless ideas from bridges to piles of balls. And then, suddenly, we had it – the image of the Parthenon (Fig 2.4) – an underpinning base of Continuous Improvement with pillars representing each of the other six elements, these supporting the roof of the whole edifice, which represented what we were trying to create: 'a professional operation'.

By coincidence, there were seven elements to the Vision and seven of us in the management team. So, what could be more appropriate than for each of us to take ownership of one of the elements? Ownership meant taking responsibility for championing that element throughout the organisation and would, in due course, require that the owner lead cross-departmental teams in action plans to realise the

Fig 2.4 - The Vision metaphor

aspirations described in that element. This idea appealed to me very strongly, because it had the additional bonus of encouraging people from different departments to work together on things that were of interest and importance to everyone. The entire Vision, with the metaphor, was set down clearly on one sheet of paper. (Appendix A). There was nothing complicated or intricate. We had described our ideal organisation in a few words that would be intelligible to anybody. But most importantly, we had built a management team with a deep understanding of what those words meant, and a real commitment to turning those words into reality.

Management Stuff

Overview

A culture change requires a framework within which changes can take place. A Vision provides such a framework. Those who are going to be involved in the change need to be closely involved in creating the

Vision, to ensure both that they understand it and that they are committed to achieving it.

The Process

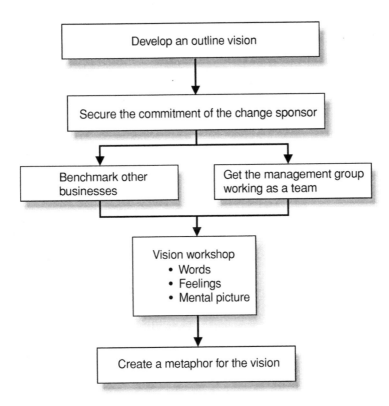

Fig. 2.5 - The visioning process

Key Points

- The change leader needs a sponsor with the power to make things happen. This usually means the person with ultimate control over the finances.

- The sponsor must be genuinely committed. A token signature on a piece of paper or lip service is worse than no commitment at all.

- If there is no crisis in the organisation, it might be necessary to create one in order to destabilise the system.

- Time must be invested in bringing the management team to the point where they want to change before trying to develop a Vision. Benchmarking other organisations or processes was highly effective in doing this.

- The management team created the Vision for themselves. The process could not be short-circuited by developing it for them.

3

Sharing the Vision

Our team of seven managers now had a very clear idea of the kind of organisation we wanted to create and we were all very keen to get on with it. However, we knew that the only way to make it happen would be to get everyone in Sellotape as excited as we were about the future. Everyone needed to understand the Vision, in exactly the same way that we did, with the same kind of imagery and emotions.

We human beings have both emotional and logical sides to our natures. Some of us appear to be driven primarily by our emotions, while others are seemingly influenced more by logic. But, what is clear, is that when something appeals to both our emotions and our intellect, it becomes a very powerful motivator indeed. Our intention in sharing the Vision was to capture both the intellect and emotions – the hearts and minds – of the whole workforce.

We were now confronted by the prospect of having to inspire the entire workforce of over 230 people to take on the Vision – rather too much of a messianic task for just seven of us. We needed to bring the first-line managers on board. These people would potentially be our most powerful allies in winning the whole organisation around. Naturally, the opinions of those whose job it is to talk to their staff every day are generally much more influential than those of any senior manager. Furthermore, if we could not succeed in winning their support, they would scupper everything we tried to do. And what chance would we then have with the others? Our change programme would sink in the mire and the mud would stick to us all. Getting these people to share our Vision was clearly the next task. Only then could we join forces to take it to the workforce as a whole.

We calculated that there were about 25 managers in positions of influence whom we thought needed to be part of the first phase of rolling out the Vision, and once again we opted for a series of workshops to accomplish this. The plan was that, after working with the first-line managers, we would enlist them to act as facilitators in phase two, which would be aimed at the shop floor.

Having learnt a little about how the event might go from our own management workshop, we used this same model as the basis from which to work. Some critical features needed to be included in the programme. These were:

- **Opening the minds** – developing an awareness of mind-sets (paradigms), and how these constrain ideas and thinking.

- **Raising the horizons** – examples of what others had achieved, to expand the concepts of what was possible.

- **Explanation of the Vision** – what it was and why we needed it.

- A display of **management commitment** to the Vision.

- An opportunity to **question and challenge** the Vision.

- **Planning** for the next stage.

We ended up running nine workshops altogether and, while they varied somewhat one from another, the formula remained largely the same. The main difference between the events for the managers and those for the shop floor was one vital element – a 'letting off steam' session for the shop floor.

Over the years, a lot of pent-up frustration had been built up on the shop floor, where the men and women were far from happy with the way they had been treated. They were disillusioned with the company and they wanted to tell any and every manager just what they thought; they were hardly in a mood to be lectured to about 'Visions' and such management crap. Besides, they had heard it all before and it had all come to nothing as far as they were concerned.

We knew that, while this frustration remained, they would not have the slightest interest in our plans. A safely valve was needed to vent these feelings. Until the pressure was relieved, there would be no space in their minds or hearts for any of our new ideas. Success, for us, would mean that the workforce would decide to channel their energy into improving the Company, rather than wasting it on blaming the management for past mistakes. Getting to this point would be tricky and would need careful handling.

We decided to extend the events for the shop floor from one day to two, to build in time for people to let off steam. Everything was designed in meticulous detail. Timings were set to the minute; the layout of the rooms and use of props planned precisely; specific responsibilities were designated for specific actions. Such a degree of planning was time consuming, but it proved essential at some of the larger events when we had up to 80 people and 9 or 10 breakout groups.

We decided to take a cross-section of staff from across all the departments to each event, because this would encourage people to think outside their normal job constraints. However, it also meant closing one half of a factory for each event, which really antagonised Sales. As for the M.D., he began to get very twitchy about the cost of having people sitting in a conference room instead of making tape. With the temperature beginning to rise, now was the time to put Franck's commitment to the test. After all, it was his money we were spending. Ever true to his word, Franck held the line. The events were on, even though it effectively cost us two full day's production, which was no small investment for a business struggling to survive.

For most of the workforce, these workshops represented the first time that they had ever been to an off-site 'learning' session and it came to symbolise a major turning point in the life of the Company. It clearly signalled to everybody in the organisation that things were changing. As part of this, we sent out personalised invitations to each employee to show that we recognised them as individuals and indicating that they had a choice to attend or not. The fact that the events were conducted during working hours meant that this choice was somewhat academic, but we wanted people to appreciate that we respected them and wanted to draw them into the process. It also served as a bit of a challenge to each and every one.

Initially, the workforce treated our proposal that they be bussed out to some activity away from the workplace with a mixture of scepticism and anxiety. After all, they had no idea what was really going on; but most came on board and the few waverers were persuaded by their managers that they should pitch in – with the 'threat' that they might even enjoy it.

We began the workshop with a warm-up exercise designed to get everyone relaxed, and to create small teams of six to eight that would work together during the event. The teams were given about 10 minutes to think up a name for themselves. To keep it light-hearted, we encouraged them to come up with something humorous. The teams then had to present themselves to the whole group, together with the reasoning behind their choice of name. This exercise had the additional purpose of introducing the participants to the idea of doing presentations to their colleagues – something they were going to be doing a lot of as the workshop progressed.

Since our sponsors' preparedness to dip into their own pockets clearly would not extend to our taking everybody out on benchmarking visits in the way that we had done for the management team, we needed another way of opening their minds to what could be achieved in our business. The answer was to use videos. We acquired Joel Barker's 'The Business of Paradigms', which explains how paradigms effect both individuals and businesses as a whole. For me, among the most memorable examples cited is the one about the watch industry. This scenario recounts that, although it was the Swiss who first invented the electronic clock, they were trapped in their own paradigm of springs and gears and failed to see the invention as a new generation of watch. The Japanese, free from this mind-set, copied the idea and the rest is history. They put the Swiss out of business.

Having seen Barker's video, the group was all fired up and ready to lay into the problems at Sellotape. The time had come for letting off steam. And what a session it was! The challenge was how to encourage people to say what they truly felt, without fear of recrimination, while simultaneously maintaining some degree of control. It was a risky strategy. We needed some kind of managed anarchy to avoid it all degenerating into a lynching party.

The solution was to create working groups focused on the problems in the business. Some groups, for example, were asked to brainstorm the things that were preventing them from doing a good job; others tackled the issue of what was wrong in the business. Still others were asked to depict their frustrations graphically on flip charts, which were posted up in the main room for all to see. Needless to say, the walls were soon well plastered with the sins and omissions

41

of the managers and owners, both past and present. Well, we had asked for it and we got it – in spades!

We were collectively accused of paying too little and expecting too much (no surprises there); of not doing what we had said we would do; of starving the business of investment; of having no concern for the workers, while driving around in expensive company cars – and of generally being a rather disreputable bunch. It was quite an experience and, as the management team in this process, we knew we had to just sit and take it on the chin, without disagreement or justification. The purpose of the exercise was to listen to their frustrations, not enter into one of those tired, old us-and-them arguments.

We carefully and deliberately acknowledged the criticisms, responding only to suggest that the resolution of all this lay in the fact that things could, should and must be better in the future. It was a clear position, and one that allowed all of the energy of the pent-up frustration to be dissipated without an argument (or a riot). At the end of these sessions one could almost see people asking themselves the question, "So what now?" The time had come to start talking about the future.

We explained what a vision was and why we needed one, and introduced the 'wedges and magnets' model, which proved very effective in giving people a frame of reference for their own situation. It helped them to understand their own frustration and confusion in the context of the state of the organisation and the way it was evolving. I believe this marked a watershed in terms of changing the culture at Sellotape. As virtually every worker in the business saw the situation, he or she was doing their very best in the job to help the Company succeed. However, their efforts were being frustrated by circumstances beyond their control. Appreciation of this allowed people to see their own problems in a new light, and provided a platform from which they had could seriously consider how they might work with us to create a better future for the Company and themselves.

Another video, this time covering the story of some British industrial miracles, helped bring the message even closer to home. One of the case studies showed the transformation of the old British Leyland into the world-class car manufacturer, Rover. (This was during the brief period when Rover was really succeeding in partnership with Honda, prior to its acquisition and subsequent sale by BMW.)

The beauty of the material was that it wasn't showing Japanese businesses on the other side of the world run by foreigners with different cultural characteristics, but companies like ours, situated just down the road. The message was clear: if other British companies had managed to reinvent themselves and become amongst the best in the world, perhaps we could do the same. And wouldn't it be nice to be part of a success story?

By this stage, we were several hours into the workshop and yet we had said absolutely nothing about what we managers had in mind for the future of Sellotape. We had taken time to prepare our audience, to help neutralise negative feelings and create some kind of a desire to emulate other successful companies. Now was the time to reveal the Vision.

This job fell to each of the managers. Their responsibility was to tell the group about their own elements by taking the pithy statement in the Vision and translating it into about ten highly illustrated slides. There was no management-speak; just plain, simple language that everyone could appreciate and relate to. Fig 3.1 shows one slide as an example. Each presentation was then rounded off with some benchmarking data, emphasising that, since others had done it, what we were talking about was indeed possible.

Presenting is not easy. It takes a lot of time to prepare the right material in the right way, and we had rehearsed until we were all confident that we could capture and hold the attention of our audience.

The night before the first workshop, we worked very late, cooped up in a small room in the Lymington factory. Dinnertime came and – when we discovered we needed to do more preparation – went. By 10 pm, we were starving. Richard Wood, the Lymington Plant Manager, was dispatched to track down some fish and chips and beer. By the time he got there even the local chippy was on the point of shutting up shop. Suffice it to say, the shared out portions of some decidedly sad-looking fish and chips in greasy paper wrappers became part of the folklore of the Ops Vision programme. Such is the lot of a senior manager during a change programme!

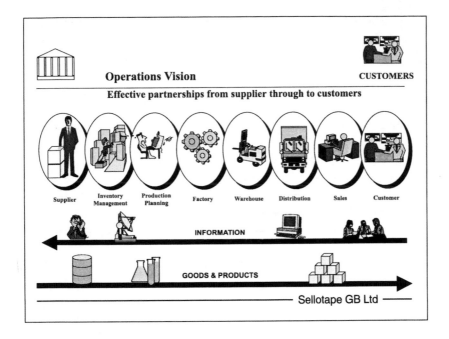

Fig 3.1 - An example of a slide used to explain aspects of the Vision

During the workshops, each manager had about 15 minutes to get his element over to the group. Then followed a breakout session in which small teams worked on what they had just heard. The idea was to give people an opportunity to talk about the content with their mates, to discuss, disagree and criticise in a safe environment. Each team had a manager or supervisor as a facilitator, briefed to provide any assistance that the team asked for. Leading or participating in the discussion was absolutely taboo. Their job was just to keep everything moving and on track, not to take control.

We maintained a strict structure for each of the tasks following on from the presentations, using techniques such as brainstorming, force field diagrams and problem ranking. At the end of the tasks, each team put together a brief presentation, which they brought back and delivered to the full group. In the early stages, many people were terrified of presenting, but in every case they quickly overcame their nerves and performed admirably. The exercises had a variety of purposes.

- First, they ensured that everyone fully understood the Vision.
- Second, they introduced workers to some of the tools that were going to be used when we started to implement the Vision.
- Third, by asking workers to do presentations, we showed that this was going to be a listening organisation in which everyone's opinion was valued.

Gone were the days when communication was just from the management to the workforce. In the new Sellotape, information was going to flow in both directions. Furthermore, we were planning to adopt presentations as a way of managing the business and the workshops provided an opportunity to introduce the idea to everyone. What pleased us all was that many individuals discovered that they were in fact rather good at presenting, and took delight in doing so. Their talents were to be put to good use in the years that followed.

One of the more off-the-wall tasks that we asked the teams to do was to perform two three-minute theatrical sketches – one depicting the present state of the organisation and the other representing the Vision. The first time we considered using this was at a small workshop for the first-line managers at our Lymington plant. The Plant manager, Richard Wood, was a down-to-earth engineer from New Zealand. He was a charismatic but somewhat traditional chap in his early 30s. Full of enthusiasm, we sat Richard down and explained what we intended doing. The angst was evident in his face. No way would his lads put up with getting involved in all this wacky stuff – "They'll hit the roof! They won't do it!" he cried. We prevailed and, sure enough, when we introduced the task to the teams, we were met by stunned silence. The seconds dragged on, feeling like hours. Then, rather stiffly, they sloped off to their corner to consider the matter. Richard, for his part, vanished from the scene and hid in his office.

Meanwhile, back in the main room, things were starting to happen. The murmur began to rise in volume and soon the whole group started to warm up amid much chuckling. It was a textbook case and we thought we would play it for all it was worth. One of us went up to Richard's office to tell him that the team was having a spot of trouble with the task, and ask him if he would please come and help us out. Richard turned pale, but bravely descended to see what he could do.

Unfortunately for him, his lads were having a great time creating a satirical sketch with Richard as the butt.

Subsequent events showed this sketch exercise to be really useful. People are prepared to say all manner of things and send messages in the form of theatre that they will not express in other ways. It proved to be yet another effective technique for venting frustrations and for learning about some of the things that actually happen on the factory floor. The most memorable sketch was one performed by a Lymington team. It went something like this:

The Scene: An imaginary production line in the factory.

An operator finds a quality problem with the product they are making.

OPERATOR: (to a co-worker) *Jane, this stuff is just not right. What do I do?*

JANE: *Call the Supervisor.*

Enter supervisor, stage left.

OPERATOR: *Here, Derek, there's something wrong with this product. What should I do about it?*

SUPERVISOR: *Dunno. Better ask Mike Green. Oi! Mike, get over here will yer?*

Enter actor with large sign hanging from his neck saying 'Mike Green, Production Manager'

PRODUCTION MANAGER: *So, what's the problem then?*

SUPERVISOR: *The profile of this stuff is outside the spec. What should we do?*

PRODUCTION MANAGER: (Studies product with furrowed brow) *Oh, sod it! It's only for caravans. The customer won't notice. Just send it.*

Howls of laughter from audience

I am sure that Mike Green never did that again!

By 'touching and feeling' the detail of the Vision and playing with it amongst themselves, the workforce soon developed a real understanding and appreciation of what the words in the Vision meant. Slowly they began to take it on board as being their own. A degree of underlying scepticism remained, but, by this stage of the workshop, we had earned enough respect from the workforce for them to give us a chance to show that this was not just another management fad.

The workshops were going very well indeed, almost better than we could have hoped; but we were very conscious of the need to take all these nice words and good feelings back to the factory and turn them into something real. Most of us have been through the experience of returning from a stimulating seminar or training, only to be told: "You can forget about that stuff here. We've got work to do." What we wanted was for everybody to go back into the workplace and start living the Vision, doing things differently. This needed a commitment from every individual.

To reach this end, we asked everyone to identify just one action that they would take when they returned to work, which would move us toward our Vision. The degree or size of the action was immaterial. It could be something as simple as tidying up a workstation. What was important was that everyone should think about doing something themselves, rather than waiting for management to take the next step. Flip charts were provided and everyone wrote down their action on a sheet and signed it, before posting it up on the walls. We had gained a public commitment to action from everyone. We had succeeded in creating a climate in which people were beginning to take responsibility for their own actions, without anyone checking on them. This had been our aim and it felt good to see it coming to life.

The seminars were a success, but not everyone was convinced that the culture change was really going to happen. There were some who believed that things were indeed going to change, but they were afraid of having their world turned upside-down. There were also a few who rather liked their world to be unhappy, so that they could grumble about management to their heart's content. Such is the way of the world. We knew that it would be impossible to convert everyone to our cause, but we felt sure that, as long as we had the support of a significant majority of the workforce, we would be successful in changing the culture.

However, we wanted to make it clear that there was no place in the new organisation for malcontents. We decided to reinforce the point, bringing in either Franck or Rory towards the end of the workshops to publicly put their stamp of approval on what we were doing. As part of their presentation, we included a slide with the following text on it:

> **You need to make a personal plan**
> **for your future**
>
> a plan to drive this Vision forward
>
> or
>
> a plan to make the best of your life
> in some other way

This became known as the FIFO message. Fit In or F--- Off. This might seem somewhat hard-nosed, given the direction we had taken; but we felt it vital to get every individual to realise that they had a choice to make: either to stay in the boat and row along with the rest of us or to get out. Sitting in our boat while secretly making holes in the bottom was not an option.

I maintain that, if we had not confronted everyone with this harsh reality, many people would have continued to operate in the same old way, unwittingly sabotaging the change process. The strategy worked. Many of those who were sitting on the fence took the decision to join us in the boat and row. A few began to make other plans for their lives.

On reflection, I believe the workshops were pivotal in the change programme. For the first time the workforce had been taken off site and been asked to participate in planning the future of the Company. It was so different from anything that they had experienced before that the event was indelibly etched into the memories of everyone who attended. From that day on, Sellotape would never be the same again.

Management Stuff

Shared ownership was achieved through cascading the Vision throughout the whole organisation. Active sponsorship was obtained from the very top and the Operations Director encouraged the management team to develop their own Vision, which was then disseminated through workshops to the first-line managers. They in turn became sponsors to the whole workforce. (Fig 3.2)

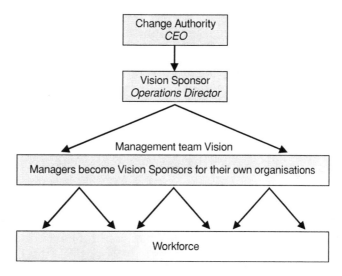

Fig 3.2 - Cascading sponsorship of the Vision

The Workshop process

A structured process was used in the workshops to overcome objections, achieve understanding and secure commitment to the Vision, as shown in Fig 3.3 overleaf.

Key Points

- Each level in the organisation was recruited as sponsors in strict order, so that each successive management layer became a sponsor of change to the next.

- Management commitment was visible at every level of the organisation.

- Off-site workshops ensured that the event was memorable and focused.

- Workshop events were carefully planned to ensure the desired outcomes were achieved, taking account of the circumstances and attitudes of the participants.

- The workshops were structured to appeal to both people's intellect and emotions.

- Implementation of the change began immediately after the workshop. Individual commitment to action was a good way to begin.

- It was made clear to everyone in the organisation that the change process required individuals to make a deliberate and active choice of whether to participate or not.

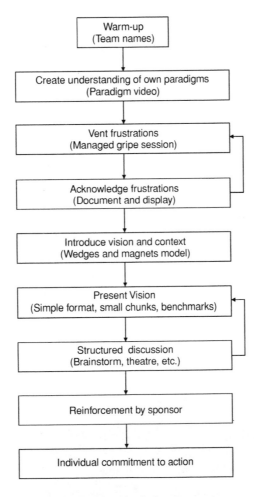

Fig 3.3 - The workshop process

4

Bringing the Vision to life

Vision without action is a daydream.
Action without vision is a nightmare.

Japanese proverb

With the workshops over, we now faced the challenge of bringing the Vision to life on the factory floor and in the offices. People were keyed up and ready to go. The time had been well spent and the enthusiasm was tangible. Shop floor and office workers alike had a mental picture of a new and exciting workplace.

It was something that had been said at one of the question and answer sessions at a vision workshop, which made me realise that we had started something that we now had to see through. An operator had stood up to say that she had heard this sort of stuff before and it had all come to nothing. What, she wanted to know, was going to be different this time. This was a key question, and I knew that my response would determine the outcome of the session.

"Well," I said, "if you are going to sit back and wait for the managers to change this business, then nothing will happen. The seven of us can't do it on our own. We have only 7 brains and 14 hands. But, I'm convinced, if we all get actively involved in pushing the changes through, we will turn this Vision into reality and create the kind of organisation we all want. The power of 230 brains and 460 hands can do it, but only if we all work at it together."

I took the same stance with the management team. If we simply stood back and hoped that the changes would happen as a result of our fine words and gestures, then the Vision would wither and die. It needed everyone to get involved. Standing around waiting for someone else to do something about making change would be disastrous. Our task was to facilitate thought and action across the whole organisation. We would need to actively involve everyone and harness the power of those 230 brains if we were to bring the Vision to life.

The watchword at the time was 'focus'. With so much that needed to be done and so many options, there was a danger of our running out of steam. We had to identify a few critical things to work on that would make a real difference and then concentrate all our energies on these.

It was like trying to eat an elephant. The only way is to select a leg and take it one bite at a time.

Having sorted out our priorities, we in the management team had to devise a structured approach to the problems that would guide people in such a way that they felt free and empowered to use their own imagination and skills to make the changes. We needed a self-reinforcing process that supported the greater purpose and was itself supported by it.

In fact, we had started identifying the critical areas soon after our own workshop, well before the roll-out vision workshops. With each of the seven managers having taken ownership of one of the elements of the vision, we had begun to develop a matrix structure for managing the organisation and the change programme. (Fig. 4.1)

This meant that each manager effectively held two responsibilities:

- his functional line job, where he was responsible for the operation of his factory or department;

- a change-leader role, in which he was responsible for driving the change of his element throughout the whole organisation.

As change leader for an element of the vision, each manager was obliged to think about Operations as a whole, always seeking where the main focus should lie. This meant, instead of it just being my job as Ops Director, we in fact had seven brains working on how to improve the effectiveness of the whole organisation.

We called the key areas that we wished to focus on 'Critical Performance Areas (CPAs)' – aspects in which we needed to perform especially well in order to make an impact on the business. After a period of individual work, we met as a team and discussed everyone's CPA at length.

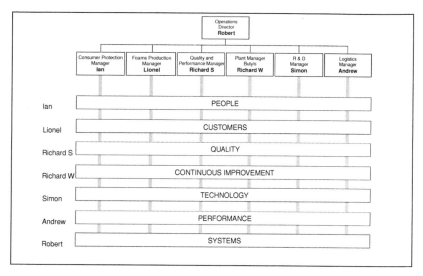

Fig 4.1 - Matrix responsibility for realising the Vision

Once again, we thrashed out the issues until we all agreed on the CPAs for each of the seven elements. This was tantamount to developing a strategic plan that would impact on every function and department. Since all the elements needed to be optimised for Operations as a whole, this meant that negotiation was the order of the day. Priorities needed to be set and agreement reached.

The exercise proved to be a valuable one, not least because it helped cement management into an even more committed team.

The Critical Performance Areas on which we settled were:

VISION ELEMENT	CPA
● People	● Freedom to act
● Customers	● Customer satisfaction
● Quality	● The cost of quality
● Systems	● Information systems
● Technology	● Manufacturing cost
● Performance	● Common performance goals

For each CPA, we then developed a SMART* objective, setting out exactly what was to be achieved and by when. SMART objectives, though well known in industry, had not previously been used in Sellotape. (They quickly flush out woolly statements of intent, as well as those objectives for which nobody can ever tell if they have been achieved or not.) These proved to be very useful throughout the programme.

The seven objectives we set up, together with the strategies describing how they would be achieved and the action schedule, constituted a very substantial programme for change. (Appendix B)

Of course, none of this is either rocket science or new. It is the sort of stuff that any trained manager would know, but it is amazing how easily one lets management discipline and concentration slip. It requires real discipline to follow through any complex set of planned actions, which is probably why managers tend to find it easier to work informally. That way we can avoid the embarrassment of not doing what we said we would. For our team, the rigour of thinking through the process and writing down the actions was part of committing ourselves to action. It also provided a series of milestones against which we, and others, could measure our progress. (An example of an action plan for one of the elements is shown in Appendix C.)

All the action plans were compiled into a little A5 booklet with about 16 pages. It was nothing fancy – just photocopies on two sides of A4, folded in half and stapled down the middle. Interestingly enough, the mere fact of reproducing the plans in booklet form made people treat them seriously. The document was seen as something special, not just as another sheet of paper to be filed. This was evident at the roll-out workshops. By waving these booklets around as evidence of our commitment, we were able to help raise the workforce's confidence in our team and in our determination to really make things happen.

Making public commitments like this was sometimes a bit scary for members of the management team. At the time, the Consumer Production department was headed up by a talented manager by the name of Ian Stringer, who had been with Sellotape through numerous

---

* An acronym for Specific, Measurable, Agreed, Realistic and Time bounded.

changes in ownership. He had never been exposed to this new-fangled approach to management. Being somewhat conservative by nature, Ian was always a little hesitant in adopting new ways of working but, once convinced that something might indeed work, he would put his heart and soul into it and deliver outstanding results.

In the early days, when the time came to commit ourselves to making the Vision happen, it was Ian who pointed out that we were going out on a limb, making very personal commitments to the people who worked for us. If, he argued, the owners or top management withdrew their support or changed direction, we would be left high and dry with our personal credibility and integrity in tatters. He was dead right and, as the longest serving manager on the team, he was taking a much greater risk than the rest of us who, being still relatively new on the scene, had less to lose. However, credit where credit is due, he took the risk and, in doing so, made a real impact on the organisation. Here was someone who was known as a solid, steady manager committing himself to fundamentally changing the way he had lived and worked for many years. It was a mark of the man and of his level of commitment to the task in hand.

Having come away from the workshops with a personal commitment to action and clear management actions, each member of the workforce was keen to get into immediate action. Everyone started to seize the opportunity to identify the things that needed fixing. This put us managers on the spot. We had to keep the momentum going, while providing the workforce with some tools with which to deal with the problems they wanted to attack. In the group exercises at the Vision workshops, we had given the shop-floor workers a taste of a few of these tools, such as brainstorming. We needed to add to these, and so devised a short training programme to equip teams to identify the causes of problems and to take effective action. The programme included a set of very basic problem-solving tools such as multi-voting, cause-and-effect diagrams, flow-charting and action scheduling. We also introduced sections on the phases of team development, as well as some principles and techniques for managing meetings. Over the next few months, we organised a series of half-day training sessions to take a large proportion of our workforce through this programme. Soon, whenever a problem raised its head in the factory or the office, the instinctive reaction was to get a small team together to sort it out by applying the various techniques.

This activity was inspiring and hugely successful, but at times there was a danger of chaos boiling over, as one team after another was set up to sort out various pet problems. It was therefore somewhat difficult to maintain a careful balance between structure and control on the one hand and our stated intent of allowing people the freedom to act on the other. What emerged was a 'hierarchy' of teamwork.

- At the top level, we had highly structured project teams, such as the one for re-implementation of our MRP system. These were large, enterprise-wide projects, often involving up to 30 people, with regular project meetings, action reviews and management reports.

- One level down were formal Continuous Improvement teams of six to eight people with stated objectives, who met regularly and documented their action plans. These were overseen by a Continuous Improvement Steering Committee which provided guidance, kept an eye on progress, and ensured we did not have more teams working than the organisation could handle. We did, after all, still need to make some tape while all this was going on.

- Underpinning the change programme were informal teams. These comprised two to four people who had decided for themselves that they wanted to work on a particular problem or improvement. They would meet and work on their project informally. There was no requirement for these informal teams to report their activity to management, but we strongly encouraged them to tell us when they had made an improvement or solved a problem. At any time, there were probably between twenty and thirty of these informal teams working across the organisation.

In an attempt to encourage those who had started to make improvements to keep on doing so, and to get others involved in the process themselves, we published details of the efforts of teams and individuals. We had, after all, committed ourselves to 'recognition of individual and team achievement'.

One of the ways we did this was by including details of

achievements in a monthly Operations brief. At the time, Sellotape GB had a process for keeping the company informed about progress. Each month the MD wrote a briefing paper that was cascaded down the formal structure by way of small group briefings. This was the ideal communications route. We started producing an Operations brief, which we disseminated on the back of the Company brief. We included some current topics of interest, but its primary purpose was to publicise improvements and to recognise those who had made them. The size or degree of the improvement was immaterial in terms of qualifying criteria for inclusion. All that mattered was that the improvement had to be in place. We wanted to trumpet results, not just bright ideas. That isn't to say that ideas were not valued, but unless they were put into effect they were virtually useless. Fig. 4.2 shows an example brief.

In our management team, there were numerous and lengthy debates about the merits or demerits of offering material rewards to those who had made improvements. Some argued long and hard that it was self-evident. As money was deemed to be the most important thing to the shop floor workers, there ought to be some kind of bonus paid. In fact, I was the only one who did not subscribe to this view and, on the basis that it was my ultimate responsibility as Ops Director, I'm afraid I insisted and prevailed. I believed then, and continue to do so now, that using money as a reward for improvements has only a very short-term impact which becomes divisive very quickly.

While it is certainly money that makes us all get out of bed and go to work every morning, I believe nevertheless that cash is not the primary motivator in the workplace. In any decent firm with a future, workers earn enough to keep a roof over their families' heads and put food on the table. The basic needs are met. Both workers and managers alike are, in my view, more driven by the need to be recognised by their peers and the powers that be, as being valuable and capable members of the enterprise.

Where the form of recognition is by cash, there is a strong tendency for people just to rapidly upgrade their standard of living, and then put their focus on boosting their own earnings to maintain their new living standards and expectations. It becomes a never-

OPERATIONS BRIEF - MARCH 95

Improvements in Action

• Eddie Carr-White and Steve Clark have developed a new layout for the Foams & Technical Tape conversion area. With Alan Long's help they have costed the changes. They are now working up a justification for the expense to put to the Board for approval.

• Dave Roberts and the Unit 15 Warehouse Team have almost completed reorganising the materials storage. The space freed up will be used to eliminate external storage, saving £700 a month.

• Lymington recorded 98.7% accuracy on a recent audit of Bill of Material accuracy. The average for the Company as a whole is 86%.

• Ken Hughes successfully transferred the slitting of 8055 from a rewind machine to the Alan Duffy, doubling the output rate.

• The Pad Shop has reduced the lead-time on pads from 15 to 13 days.

• A modification to one of the pad shop presses costing £5600 has reduced the changeover time from 25 to 7 minutes. Laurie Oliver came up with the idea and justified the investment.

• Sharon Ramsey has developed a process and a simple form, which ensures we know the tolerances the customers require before we confirm that we can produce a sample.

Training Highlights

• Paul Wright, the QA manager at Lymington, is drawing up a 2 day 'CI Team Leader' course. It will be piloted at Lymington, and then extended to Dunstable.

• A 'Train the Trainer' course is being run this week by Eddie Carr-White for 4 people at Dunstable.

• All the Open College course students at Dunstable scored either 'credit' or 'distinction' for their last assignment.

Investment

• A new AMK mixer costing £280,000 has been approved for Lymington. Besides giving us the ability to take the oldest mixer out for rebuilding, the new machine includes new technology that reduces the mixing time by 30%.

• We have ordered new printers costing £13,000 for Foams production.

• After the successful trial of the Kienzle equipment for recording machine performance in the Consumer plant, a further 4 units were ordered last week, at a cost of £11,000.

Bad News

Waste levels in Foams production, and Lymington are running high and costing us money. We need to :

      i) Measure how much waste we are producing.
      ii) Find out what the major causes of waste are.
      iii) Get to grips with the problems and eliminate them.

'A Professional Operation'

ending quest that shifts the focus away from the continuous improvement. Besides making it difficult to set wage levels, it can also sow the seeds of discontent among the workforce and cause the flow of improvements to dry up. By contrast, there is almost infinite resource available in any organisation for meeting individuals' need for recognition, with a much lower risk of disillusion, unhappiness and, over time, a spiralling wage bill.

In the Ops Vision programme, we never once paid any cash rewards. By taking the trouble to publicise who had done good work; giving individuals forums in which to talk about what they had achieved; and providing opportunities for individuals and teams to have new experiences or develop their capabilities, we achieved our aim of encouraging participation and commitment. This isn't to say that there wasn't a low-level grumble that financial recognition would have been nice. However, the level of morale remained high and the flow of improvements never dried up.

Developing the capabilities of the people in the business was probably the single most effective factor in bringing the Vision to life; and the most significant tool we had at our disposal was the Open College Supervisory Management Programme, which we came upon by accident. The Open College is a registered charity that provides a range of vocational programmes at relatively low cost. Of the options available, the supervisory management programme seemed to meet our needs in that it covered a range of basic team and management skills. The course operated on the basis of a lot of extra-mural work by the students, with a monthly one-day workshop, supported by individual tutoring sessions lasting an hour or so. The course was certainly demanding, with a high time commitment demanded from the student, since most of the work was done outside of working hours. At £1,000 per student for the full nine-month programme, we thought it represented very good value.

We needed a minimum of eight students to run a programme and were unsure as to what the response would be. We put a notice up on the boards, briefly outlining what the programme entailed, and asked for anyone interested to submit their name. We were absolutely stunned when more than 80 applications came in. However, the maximum number we could accommodate on the programme was 14, which meant that we were faced with a new problem – how to reduce the number without causing too many people too much disappointment. It was evident that there was a real desire amongst the workforce to learn. This was now a totally different body of people from the demoralised bunch I had first met.

We invited all the applicants to a meeting at which we explained that the course represented a lot of work, that they would have to do most of it in their own time, and that on completion of the training there would be no extra money nor promotion. At the end of the presentation, we added that those who were still interested should complete an application form, which we asked them to collect from an office at the far end of the building. Amongst other things, the form asked applicants to outline what benefits they expected to gain from going on the course and how they thought this would benefit the company. Having completed the application, they also needed to get a signature from their manager. Even after putting all these obstacles in the way, we still got about 20 applications. Ultimately, in order to get the number down to 14, we asked the managers to interview all the applicants from their respective departments, to select the best candidates on the basis of who might benefit most and have the highest chance of success. We did, however, guarantee places on a subsequent course to the six who missed out on the first one.

What this lesson taught me was just how much scope and desire for personal development there is deep down amongst shop-floor workers. The challenge for managers everywhere is to find ways of tapping into this rich seam of talent.

The programme benefited the students themselves, their colleagues, their supervisors and the company as a whole from the very outset. Each student had an individual mentor, who was a supervisor or manager from his workplace. This drew a further fourteen people into discussing the course material and woke the mentors up to what they did not know. Each module on the course required the student to work on a practical situation in the workplace, which in turn drew the student's workmates into talking about issues and how to resolve them. All of this focus and activity meant small improvements were constantly being made and it kept up the momentum. For the final stage of the course, each student had to carry out an investigation into an actual problem or opportunity in the workplace, and then present their findings and recommendations to the directors and managers. Once again, we were all flabbergasted. The quality of the projects was outstanding – so much so that we adopted almost all the recommendations and put projects in place to implement them. We also reviewed progress on a regular basis to make sure that it really happened. (Appendix D)

All our students passed, with several of them gaining merit awards at a national level and, encouraged by this, we ran the programme twice more in the next two years, qualifying some sixty people in total.

Now that we were really motoring, we wanted to improve the working environment to reinforce the impression that headway was being made. The first improvement addressed housekeeping in the factory. After all, no professional likes working in dirty or untidy conditions and it is certainly not good for safety and efficiency. To grapple with this particular nettle, we devised a competition among departments to win the housekeeping trophy. The unfortunate department that came last would receive a booby-prize trophy – a battered jam tin mounted on a piece of wood, awarded in perpetuity. Competition can be divisive, however – something we were very keen to avoid. The secret behind the success of this competition lay in having a judging panel made up of representatives from each department. This way everyone had a role in deciding on the winner and there was no possibility of a charge of unfairness or poor judgement being levelled. An added benefit was that each representative got to see what the others were doing to improve their situation, which provided an opportunity to go one better and perhaps seize the prize.

One thing we had said to the workforce was that we valued everyone in the organisation equally. Naturally, some had rare skills and so earned better pay; but we maintained that they were neither better, nor more valuable as a person, than anyone else. What flew in the face of this, however, were the car parking arrangements. A separate area was reserved for the senior managers and the directors, who generally rolled in later than everyone else and parked closest to the door.

We knew that this privilege needed overturning for credibility's sake. It was an issue for Rory (who by then had taken on the mantle of M.D.) to resolve. We persuaded him to change the parking rule to one of first-come-first-served. I certainly wasn't flavour of the month amongst some of the other directors, who were seriously miffed given that they often ended up having to park miles away from the office. They could be heard muttering under their breath about how they were losing the privileges they had worked so hard to get. The rest of the workforce, however, were simply astonished. Although no one actually openly expressed this view, opinion has it that this act represented a very powerful signal that things were indeed changing.

Management Stuff

Approach:
A project was set up to implement the changes, with the work initiated immediately after the workshops to keep up the momentum. Actions were focused on a few clearly defined objectives. Training and development was a key enabler of change. Continuous recognition of achievement supported and encouraged desirable behaviour.

Critical Success Factors:

- Application of the 80/20 principle to determine the 20% of actions that would deliver 80% of the changes.

- Management team agreement on critical success factors.

- SMART management objectives.

- Structured management action plans.

- Workers involved in activities that were previously the preserve of management.

- Small but highly visible improvements in the working conditions.

- Managers seen to be living the values in the Vision.

- Public acknowledgement of achievement.

- Implementation through a mix of formal projects and informal project teams.

Recognition and reward:

Idea generation and implementation of improvements can be made a feature of an organisation without financial incentives. The higher level factors, such as recognition and team socialisation, are powerful motivators that outlast monetary rewards.

5

Some of the Results

About six months into the Vision programme, we were sitting around in one of our weekly management meetings and got to talking about what we had actually achieved to date. It felt as though we were rowing through treacle, doing a lot of hard work but getting nowhere fast. We agreed on an action point, which was minuted as follows:

List all the improvements made in your area over the past six months under the headings:

- Problem or opportunity

- Improvement process

- Results

Action: All Ops Management Team members

Due date: Next Friday

I looked around. On everyone's face, mine include, I was sure, was an expression which showed a mixture of external calm and internal panic. Oh my God! we seemed to be exclaiming to ourselves, where on earth am I going to find something to report back on? I knew we would all have one or two changes that we could list, but they hardly represented anything like a worthwhile report.

The following Friday arrived and we met as usual. After the customary review of the week's events we each started to report on our action point. What a surprise! Everyone had come equipped with a long list of improvements that they had identified. We ended up listing a total of 69 improvements that we knew of. (Appendix E shows just one page of the summary we compiled.) When we had had to sit down and think about it all, the list of the changes that had indeed taken place had just came flooding into our heads. Because we had been so close to things day to day, we had simply not noticed just how much had in fact been changing around us. The improvements had just crept up on us, much in the same way that the hands of a clock move incessantly, but scarcely perceptibly.

Some of the improvements had been minor and cosmetic, such as the packaging technologist obtaining a cupboard for storing her samples, instead of cluttering up the office with them. Others were significant in terms of their impact on the business. For example, product changeover times on the butyl extruder at our Lymington plant had been reduced by 50% through the work of a Continuous Improvement team. But there was a common factor running through all the changes – each and every one had moved us another step towards the Vision.

In May 1995, I was asked to present our results to the Group MD's meeting. The slides I presented are shown in Figs. 5.1 and 5.2, revealing some of the more impressive improvements that we had made. So, things were indeed progressing well; but I still had some doubts about just how deeply the culture change had penetrated into the organisation.

The first time I started to really believe that we were beginning to make a difference was when I was doing a bit of managing by walking around in the factory. I stopped to chat to an operator running a slitter that cut the large Jumbos into smaller rolls of tape. He told me that he had just installed a switch that would allow him to turn off the core feed conveyor when the slitter stopped. This, he explained, would prevent damage to those cores held on the conveyor. I was chuffed to bits. True, the modification would not do much for the fortunes of the company overall, but it was the process and the return on investment that excited me. Here was a man who had been running this machinefor years, just because we paid him to do so. As a result of the Vision and the work we had all done, he had started to take an active interest in what he was doing. He had identified an area of waste, found a way of improving the situation, and made the alteration himself.

Operations Review - Dunstable & Lymington

A Professional Operation

Continuous Improvement - Some Examples

- **A modification to a pad press costing £5600 has reduced changeover time from 25 to 7 minutes**
  - Pad Shop Manager visited Germany and machine supplier. Saw the idea and justified the investment.

- **A change to the system of handling jumbos into the hot box reduced labour cost by £7000 per year**
  - An operation on the Supervisory training programme did this as a course assignment.

- **The waste from the Hot Melt Coater was reduced by £102,000 in 1994 compared to 1993**
  - A team improved operating procedures and developed a method of cleaning the die lips.

Operations Review - Dunstable & Lymington

A Professional Operation

Continuous Improvement - More Examples

- **We now use plastic cores on the Hot Melt Coater, which can be recycled. As a follow-on we are working with our film supplier to use the same cores, so that all cores are recycled.**
  - Operator suggested using cling-film on the core which eases stripping of the tape at the end of a run.

- **An investment of £3.48 for a switch on a core loader is saving £500 p.a. in damaged cores.**
  - Made operators aware of cost of core damage and empowered them to make changes.

- **Introduced one-piece cheek-plates for bobbins saving £4,500 p.a.**
  - The operator suggested eliminating plastic inserts. The Packaging Technologist worked with him to develop it into a working solution.

Figs 5.1 and 5.2 - Presentations to Group MD's meeting

The monetary investment had been all of £3.48 for a new switch! The annual saving was about £500 in reduced damage, which was a very attractive return. But, most important, this person now had a sense of pride about what he had done. He was no longer 'just an operator', who ran a machine every day because he was paid to do so. He had become an active participant in something at a much higher level – someone helping to realise our Vision of becoming 'A Professional Operation'.

On yet another of my walkabouts, I was made aware that the Pad Shop team had been working on the layout of the shop. So, off I went to see how they were getting on. In the pad shop, we cut little gaskets, using an array of small presses. It was the sort of shop where it was easy for managers to try out new ideas for layout, since the machines were comparatively easy to move and the whole department, which was run by a team of 10 women, was situated away from the rest of the plant. One of the operators called me over.

"I've been here 15 years," she said, "and they have changed the layout in this place at least half a dozen times. This is the first time I have been asked what I think about the proposed layout. This time we have something that actually works better for all of us."

It transpired that not only had she been asked; in fact the team had learnt how to draw up a layout. They had, moreover, costed out the move, argued the case for the investment and arranged for the all the work to be done. They even had the walls painted in the Sellotape colours and created a new Rest Area. Feeling great, I sought out the department manager to discuss how things had gone. He was equally delighted, remarking that the most difficult thing for him had been to avoid behaving like a traditional manager and taking over from the team. His self-control had paid off handsomely. (Fig. 5.3)

When we set out on the journey toward our Vision, we concentrated on the processes, making things better and encouraging people to improve their own working lives. We deliberately steered clear of demanding results, avoiding the usual management trick of getting people to commit up front to how much money they were going to save over the next year. We adopted this approach largely as an act of faith: that if we did the 'right things', the hard benefits, in terms of money, would naturally flow as a result. In the early stages

67

Problem	Shop cluttered, high work in progress, poor work flow
Team	Three pad-shop operators, the section leader and two operators from the departments that provided the pad shop with materials
Management role	Provided time and resources Avoided interfering
Process	Developed new layout, working through three revisions to get it right Designed colour scheme Obtained costs Developed justification for expenditure Team controlled and managed the work
Results	An environment of which the operators are proud Reduced work in progress Productivity up 41% on previous year, saving £40,000 p.a. Cost - £3,000

Fig 5.3 - Pad shop reorganisation

therefore, we had made no attempt to quantify what was being achieved in financial terms. Indeed the summary of our first 'what-have-we-achieved' review did not contain one single pound sign.

Up until then, our sponsors, Franck and Rory, had gone along with this leap of faith, but after a while, they began to crave some tangible monetary benefit out of all this 'fluffy' visioning stuff we had spent so much time working on. Franck expressed his concern that we were creating a kibbutz – a society where everyone works together for the benefit of the community but creates no wealth outside that society.

"Where is 'the beef' (the benefit to the business) from all this wonderful activity?" he asked. I felt a touch put out by his attitude: after all, it had been he who had originally asked for a change in the culture and we had delivered. There was no argument about that. The organisation was now focused on improvement and people were once again becoming proud to work for Sellotape. But I knew where he was coming from and recognised that we needed to move to the next phase and deliver 'the beef', if we were going to maintain the confidence and support of our sponsors.

In fact, we did not have to change what we were actually doing. We just started to put a monetary value on the results, which by this time was not difficult. Furthermore, we reckoned that the workforce both needed, and had the right, to know about the results of their activities. We were already being open about the financial performance of the Company: the sales figures were posted on the notice board every week and the profits reported each month in the Company brief. The entire workforce was involved in making improvements and naturally enough, they were keen to see what their own contributions meant to the overall profit of the company. From then on in, pound signs were to be found in great numbers in the report on improvements in the monthly brief.

We were, however, careful to be conservative in our estimation of the value of improvements. We were all thoroughly opposed to developing a 'bullshit' culture for practical and moral purposes. We also resisted all requests to add up the benefits as an indication of the expected profit improvement.

By the very nature of the programme, many of the initiatives and projects overlapped and so there was a degree of double counting. As far as we were concerned, this was not an issue. Indeed, we wanted people working on problems from several angles. It was this approach that would produce the best results. Despite the new emphasis on monetary results, we continued to work on the processes and the softer issues, since we were certain that we would need to keep the momentum going across all the elements of the Vision if we hoped to deliver long-term financial returns.

The ultimate indicator of progress, for us, was how the people viewed it all, and so we decided to conduct an attitude survey to get a measure of this. The question was whether to tackle it ourselves – we had after all done practically everything else without help from outside, so why not this?

In the end, however, we decided to get a firm of professionals in to do the job. While we paid out a bucketful of money, I maintain that the benefits far outweighed the cost. Firstly, any fear that individual responses might be reported to management was removed, which meant that we were more likely to get honest feedback. Second, the processes for gathering and evaluating the responses were much better than anything we could have come up with.

During the survey, we had an amusing diversion at the Lymington plant. The response-gathering process involved having a researcher from the survey company getting groups of about fifteen employees together in a room, where they were asked questions to which they responded by pressing buttons on an electronic pad. During one of these sessions, a couple of lads came into the factory off the street looking for jobs, only to find themselves being herded into the survey room along with our people. Naturally, the researcher did not know who they were and assumed they belonged to us, while the group thought they were a control brought in by the researcher. What the interlopers thought of this strange selection process, we never found out, but fortunately the error was discovered amidst much hilarity and the results were adjusted to eliminate the responses of our uninvited friends.

We did in fact carry out two surveys, the first shortly after the launch of the Vision and the second about fifteen months later. Some examples of the results are shown in Figs 5.4 and 5.5 opposite.

About one year into the programme, the management team had another 'so-what-have-we-achieved' session. The list looked remarkably different to the one we had drawn up six months earlier. This time, pound signs were liberally strewn around the summaries. There were fewer small projects, but a greater number of formal Continuous Improvement teams working on substantial change issues. But to my mind, the most significant difference was captured in one comment:

"Today, the workforce sees 'helping the company to save money' as a good thing to be doing."

I circulated the summary of our 1995 review to Rory. He scribbled on the document: "There is some excellent stuff in here. It proves that, even without formal goals, people want to make changes. We are so far ahead from where we started."

We were finally delivering 'the beef', repaying our sponsors for the faith they had shown in us.

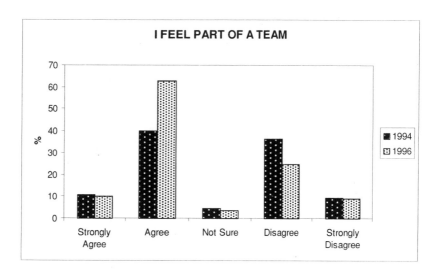

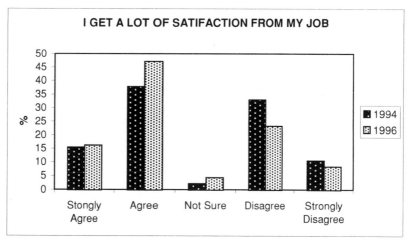

Figs 5.4 and 5.5 - Example results from the attitude survey

Management Stuff

The results had little to do with management, but much to do with the workforce.

Key Lessons:

- Start by fixing the processes.

- Don't stifle enthusiasm by immediately demanding financial returns.

- Be conservative when calculating benefit values.

- There will be some double counting of benefits of overlapping projects. Don't expect the profit to increase by the sum of the individual benefits.

- Small benefits are as valuable as the large ones in terms of their impact on the culture.

- And a repeat of an earlier point, because of its importance: Recognise and celebrate achievement.

6

"Get the stock down"

It was with feelings of great unease that I entered the office. Franck and Rory had called me in and as soon as I had pushed the door open, I knew that life was about to change once again.

The two of them sat there stony faced and I steeled myself for the onslaught. "We want to see the stocks reduced by £1million within the next 60 days," said Franck. Clearly the lack of progress at reducing the mountain of stock in the business had finally got to them and time had run out.

When they had taken over the business, Franck and Rory had found the inevitable stock surplus that exists in badly run operations. The stock value was around £6 million and it had remained more or less steady at that level. Rory had identified this as an area needing attention early on, both as a source of cash and as a resource drain, but none of initiatives launched to date had made any inroads into the situation. The usual outcome – a list of slow-moving and redundant stocks – was handed to the salesmen who were despatched together with exhortations to sell the stuff. Naturally, the results were lamentable. The lists comprised pages of items and nobody really understood the details. Furthermore, salesmen stood to earn less commission on the slow-moving stock, which was being offered at a discount. More important still, they also stood the risk of making enemies of otherwise satisfied customers by selling them something that might just turn out to be dodgy or, worse still, the wrong product. And finally, to snuff out any residual incentive that might have survived in the salesmen, the management in Sales considered surplus stock not as their problem but as that of Production. As a result, they provided little or no leadership or motivation to Sales staff to clear it out. Then again, to give them their due, on the few occasions that

Sales had actually found a buyer for some redundant stock, it usually turned out that the product did not exist, could not be found, or, if indeed the product did materialise, the quality was so poor that it was not fit to be sent out. This left Sales with the unpleasant task of having to unravel a deal which they had laboriously set up, leaving red faces and frayed nerves all over the place. It was hardly a surprise that the stock remained stubbornly in the warehouse!

Reducing the stock by some £1million in two months was a tall order but, after a brief discussion on the previous failures, I said, "Let me think about it for a day and I'll come back to you on what I need to get the job done." I left with my mind in overdrive and wandered down to my office. How the hell do I get a handle on this one? I asked myself. It would be a real challenge. But that was why I had taken on the job, wasn't it? Still, having been involved in the most recent list generation exercise myself, I had a good idea of the magnitude of the problem. The issues were these:

- There were so many items in stock, each with its own history and matrix of possibilities, that it was impossible for people to develop a clear picture of the problem as a whole and to decide what to do about it. Faced by a 20-page list of slow-moving stock in fine print, any normal manager would take one look at it and put it in the 'too difficult' pile, where it would stay until everybody lost interest. Then he could safely throw it away.

- The lines of responsibility for controlling the flow of material into the business and for dealing with stock problems were, at best, blurred. It was always someone else's problem. Absolutely no one accepted that inventory, or any part of it, was his problem.

- The problems were of such a nature that no single individual could resolve them on his own. It would take a minimum of two functions working together to identify the best way of removing the obstacles to finding ways of moving the stock.

- The process needed support and commitment from board level and from the head of every function.

After a fitful night's sleep, I went in to see Franck.

"It's possible," I said, "but I'll need your help with two things. I need your influence to ensure that I get the full support of the UK Board in this. They're going to have to allocate people to the project and get involved themselves when necessary. Also, I will need someone on a temporary basis with the intellect and drive to manage the process."

This, I explained, was because an existing manager with normal responsibilities would be distracted by the daily crises and priorities, and so would inevitably allow the pace of the project to slip. What we needed was someone who had nothing else to worry about, and the ability to get action going on the things he was worried about. Franck looked grim for a fleeting moment. Then his usual determined expression returned. He took a deep drag on a Gauloises and nodded his agreement.

The first step in tackling the problem was to understand what made up this £6 million mountain. Only then would we be in a position to work out what to do with it. I sat down at my desk for a few hours to think about where the stuff had come from and what possible avenues there were to move it out of the business. I then divided the inventory into various categories, before identifying how we might shift each one. (Fig 6.1)

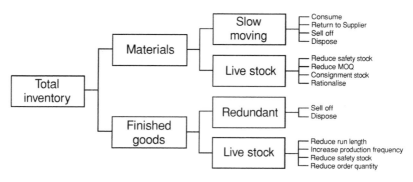

Fig 6.1 - Analysis of inventory and potential options for reducing the total

The two obvious components were raw materials and finished goods. In both, there would be a certain amount of stock that was necessary for the normal running of the business. Besides that, as in most companies, we would probably be carrying quite a bit of excess 'just-in-case' stock. Both the 80/20 rule and my own experience tended to confirm that, usually, there is far too little of the few fast runners and a massive surplus of those that are hardly ever required. In addition there would inevitably be loads of stock that was redundant, either because the customer for whom it was made had stopped buying, or because the material had been replaced.

By approaching the problem this way, I soon realised that there were a number of alternatives and previously unexplored avenues for clearing out both the raw material and the finished goods. Curiously, we had never really sought to return material to suppliers before. This seemed to be a potentially easy and quick way to make progress. Also, the deeper I dug, the more I learnt about how things had conspired against the Company in the past. For example, safety stock levels and minimum production runs had always been set without considering the real cost of inventory. Here was an opportunity to make improvements, even though the benefits would take some time to come through.

Having got some idea of the nature of the stock piled up in the warehouse, I also needed to think about stock movements into the business. After all, it would be ridiculous moving stock out of the warehouse if this merely meant triggering new orders to fill the space made available. It was time to tackle the question of material and product flows, and define the responsibilities to ensure that specific individuals felt accountable for controlling what ended up on the shelves. (Fig. 6.2)

This move towards defining responsibility among the various people met with a certain amount of resistance. Deciding how much to buy or produce is a complex decision requiring information from many sources, including sales forecasts, costings, production data and so on. Clearly, the ability of one individual to collect and manage all these variables is limited; so, on the face of it, I was being unreasonable in wanting to dump the problem in any one person's lap. However, in an environment where everybody considered inventory to be everyone else's problem, we had to get some kind of accountability. I explained this to my colleagues, which softened the blow a little, reasoning that, though not a perfect solution, it would start moving us away from the 'shrug-your-shoulders' culture that currently existed whenever the wheels fell off the cart.

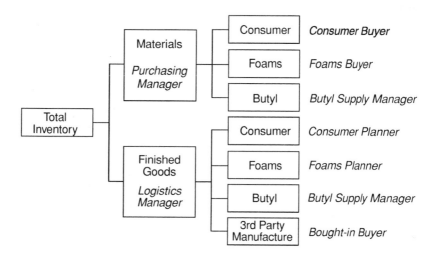

Fig 6.2 - Definition of responsibility for inventory segments

To get some early successes under our belts, which always raises morale and gets the process moving, I decided to focus attention on a few high-value items and ignore just about everything else. In this way, the project team (which still had to be set up) would be able to grasp the full implications of issues surrounding each item. What needed to be understood was:

- what the products or materials were
- what they could be used for
- where they came from
- what other possibilities existed for their use
- and, if the worst came to the worst, where we could get the best scrap value.

Speed was of the essence. By concentrating on a few select items, we were confident that we could get the rapid results we needed to give the project credibility and to get the team motivated. It was essential that people realised that dealing with this inventory monster was not in fact impossible.

Having sorted out a plan of attack, I set to building my project team. Since every function in the business can and does influence the stocks in the warehouse in some way or other, I sought to have representatives from each of the disciplines in the team. Furthermore, these team members needed to have the authority to take decisions and get things done. This team could not be a toothless tiger; it had to be able to bite and bite hard.

I gathered a group of seven people together. Purchasing and Production Planning were well represented, with members from each of the factory units. Sales included the forecaster, a Sales manager and one of the Customer Service staff. The final member was an accountant, whose job it was to keep score and to help identify the cost or potential benefits of our actions. We also established an informal Steering Group, comprising the MD, the directors responsible for Sales and Finance, and myself as head of Operations. Our job was to provide the executive support and drive that would be necessary to give the team the power it needed. Franck was also drafted in as the sponsor of the exercise. This helped to concentrate the minds of my fellow Board members, who, because they also laboured under the misapprehension that the stock problem was someone else's responsibility, were a little reluctant to get involved. But there was another factor at play here. People are often disinclined to play a part in any project that has the taint of previous failed attempts. However, since Franck clearly thought it important, they decided that they had better show willing.

All that was needed now was a team leader who could devote his whole being to this project. We employed a junior consultant from one of the major consulting houses, where I had a personal relationship with one of the partners. By calling in a few favours I was able to negotiate the services of a bright young consultant with the right attributes for our project at a good rate, without also having to pay for partner supervision and the usual contribution to the glossy corporate headquarters' building.

With the team established, we needed a process for taking decisions and ensuring that they would be carried out. We also identified a few basic principles around which to build the process. These were:

- a high degree of visibility of the issues, actions and results
- rapid decision making

- the team's role was to solve problems, not to add to them
- roles and accountability were to be clearly defined
- rapid action, with strict adherence to deadlines
- progress was to be tracked
- recognition of success.

We decided that the team would meet every day for 10 to 15 minutes, in order to maintain the pace and to ensure that we could correct any mistakes or wrong decisions immediately. We then came up with the idea of displaying everything about the project on an office wall. This was to keep the project profile high, while helping provide a visible project-tracking tool.

For greatest effect, we took over a complete wall in the main office area. There we created a project board with sections marked off for 'problems', 'actions', 'successes', 'progress' and 'long-term issues and opportunities'. (Fig.6.3) Because of the prominence of this board, the whole exercise ultimately became known as 'The Wall Project'.

Since the wall we chose was along the corridor that most of the office staff used when going to the canteen, it was virtually impossible for anybody to walk by without looking at what was happening. Soon, even those who were not involved in the project took an interest in how things were going, and thus the whole company was able to remain in touch with the progress we were making.

Information was displayed on the Wall using Post-it notes – one per issue. These were stuck up in the 'problems' area. The team then discussed the nature of the item, the quantity, why it was surplus to our requirements and what could be done with it. Members of the team would then volunteer to take responsibility for carrying out the agreed actions and a completion date was set. The original 'problem' note was then updated with the action detail and moved across to the 'action' area of the Wall. Once the action had been completed (which meant that some of the inventory had been cleared), the outcome was written on the Post-it note, before it was moved to the 'successes' column. And there it stayed. The more successes, the more notes built up in the column, making progress very visible. However, to be a little more precise about tracking the progress, we recorded the cumulative reduction in the inventory value on a bar chart displayed at the end of the Wall (Fig.6.4).

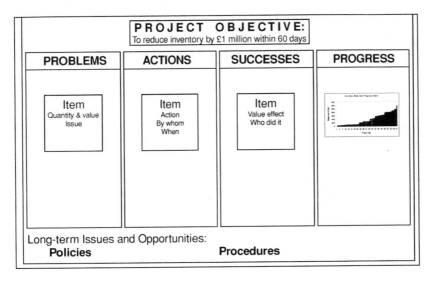

Fig 6.3 - The Wall

As each problem moved across to the 'action' section, a new item would be introduced into the process.

With the time allowed for completing actions being kept very tight, we were able to identify any lack of progress very quickly, and institute remedial action immediately. A 'success' was only counted

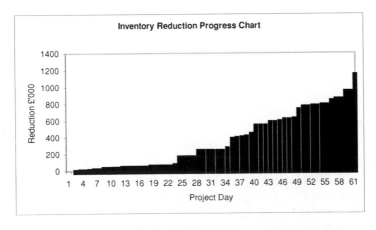

Fig 6.4 - Inventory reduction progress chart

when goods were dispatched against an order, or physically removed for disposal. (Fortunately, we had a provision to cover write-off and disposal of material as a last resort.)

To focus the team's work and get the maximum effect, we started the process by targeting a few high impact items. The original idea was to begin with between 10 and 20 items in the 'problems' area and then to add more as these first items began to be moved on to the 'action' phase. Initially, we looked only at items for which we had more than 12 months' cover and which were on the books at more than £7,000 in value. As the weeks went by, these limits were gradually reduced until, by the end of the project, we reached five months' and £5,000. We also made sure that we were never dealing with more than 60 items in total at any one time.

Senior management's role in the process was to provide support and drive, and to take any major decisions that would have a significant effect on the business. When necessary, we invited some of the Directors to attend the daily meeting. This was in order to get them involved in actions which were not moving fast enough, or to provide a boost at moments when progress seemed slow and the team appeared to be flagging.

While all this inventory reduction work was being carried out, we also sought to address the reasons for the original stock mountain. This meant tackling some of the underlying decision-making processes and rules, as well as re-examining safety stocks and minimum order quantities. The safety stock levels had been established when the computerised accounting system had been installed many years before. At that time, the emphasis had been on ensuring that the business never ran out of material, no matter what the circumstances. With such a range of items, reworking the stock levels for each would have been time consuming and difficult. It was time we couldn't spare. On the other hand, we couldn't afford to get it wrong, both for the credibility of the exercise and for the safety of the business. We needed to come up with an effective and quick process for establishing realistic stock levels without risking anything going wrong.

The solution was a one-time fix. We arranged for the computer to examine the minimum stock recorded for each item over the previous three months, to divide this quantity by two and then to deduct the result from the reorder point. (See Fig.6.5 overleaf for a graphic representation.) It was a somewhat rough and ready measure, but it took only a matter of days to put in place and, most importantly, it worked. Purchase orders for materials and demand for production fell noticeably over several weeks.

Minimum order quantities were tackled in an equally radical manner. Previously, production runs on foams had been set at a minimum of 1000 metres in order to minimise waste. This rule was abolished. Instead, we put in place a decision-making process that determined economic production runs for each product, by balancing the cost of changeover, waste and the inventory. The effect was dramatic. On some product lines, because of extremely high changeover costs, we actually extended the run length. Other runs were significantly reduced. With a few products, we found to our horror that the length of run needed to make them profitable represented more than their total annual sales! Needless to say, production on these lines was stopped.

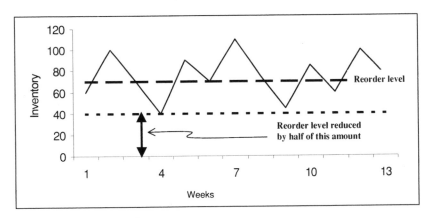

Fig 6.5 - Reorder levels were reduced by half the minimum recorded stock

As so often happens in tackling a major systematic problem such as this, the results were slow in appearing. After two full weeks of concentrated effort we had only cleared about £65,000. The £1million target began to look like an impossibility. Motivation began to dip and with it went morale. We needed a success. Our 'saviour' came in the guise of something called 'gaffer tape'. There was a veritable pile of it, and it was so old that glue had started to ooze from the sides of the rolls. There was no way that we could sell it as standard product. Only one course of action was available to us – to sell it off as a job lot to a scrap merchant at a price well below the book value. It all disappeared in a week, marking the first real kick in our progress-tracking graph on day 24. This lifted the team's spirits and more successes followed soon afterwards. We also had the occasional 'win', which helped to offset the loss on the gaffer tape. One of the team, for example, discovered a perfect roll of very costly material in the stores that did not exist in the books. Finding this lost treasure alone netted us a cool £25,000 in recovery costs.

As the chart shows, the results grew exponentially through the project and, suffice it to say, we reached our target and beat it. But our successes did not end there. The work that had been done continued to yield benefits. Over the two weeks following the 60-day deadline, the stocks fell by a further £400,000, as the results of the work done during the life of the project continued to bear fruit.

Flushed with our success, we terminated the project, remembering to close it down formally. This proved very useful. It made us think about what had to be done to prevent the stock building again once we returned to normal operations. As it happened, we never looked back. With the new understanding and discipline, a 'Phase 2 Wall Team' was set up by the original team to continue the work, with the result that inventory levels continued to fall over the next two years, while customer service improved to unprecedented levels.

Management Stuff

Approaching projects:

In projects such as these, a vehicle is needed to bring together the multitude of variables and factors that lie at the root of the problem. The goal needs to be clear and top management support is vital. To achieve the goal, the information required must be accurate and thoroughly understood by all involved. To ensure this accuracy and consistency, there should be only one source of information. An effective multi-functional team should then be set up, with the authority to act independently in terms of taking and carrying out the relevant decisions and actions.

'The Wall' represented an effective way of bringing all these factors together. (Fig.6.6)

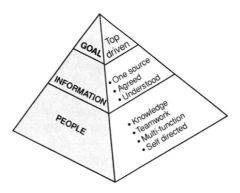

Fig 6.6 - The Wall as a focal point for issues and drivers

The process:

A well-defined process was needed to get from the start point, i.e. the problem, to the desired end point, i.e. the problem resolved. (Fig.6.7)

Critical Success Factors:

- Clear objectives with a finite target and a time limit.

- Top management support and involvement.

- Multi-functional team representing all disciplines involved in managing the supply chain.

- Clear responsibility for action.

- Dedicated resource to lead the project.

- Visible process and progress tracking.

- Recognition of successes.

- Formal closure of the project to identify failures, successes and follow-through actions.

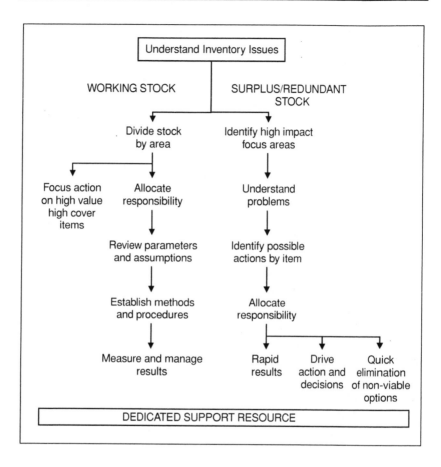

Fig 6.7 - Project process overview

7

Making the Supply Chain Work

On the day that I started at Sellotape, I was assailed by virtually every manager in the business complaining about the customer service or, more accurately, the lack of it. At the time, 'customer service' meant simply delivering what the customer ordered more or less when he expected it. There were no refinements that one would normally label as customer service. It was just deliver the goods! The organisation was simply incapable of meeting orders in full and on time. In fact, when a measure of delivery performance was established, we found that we were only dispatching in the region of 40% of orders when we were supposed to. Needless to say, our customers could hardly be described as delighted.

For me this was a real problem. Having been branded 'a big hitter from a multinational', I was expected to be able to fix everything within a few days or weeks. Why else were they employing me? That was the gist of the expectation, but for me it was evident that, if this is what they were hoping for, there were going to be a lot of disappointed people around. I had no magic to fix such problems. There were deep-rooted and fundamental issues across the company that needed to be addressed, before we could hope for happy customers.

Day-to-day operations were beset by incessant crises. Forecasting of customer demand was a finger-in-the-air job. "How do we know what the customers are going to order?" was the standard cry. "This business is different," everyone said. "We have to be flexible to satisfy our customers." Having nothing upon which to predict demand, the buyer bought the materials that he guessed might be needed, based on the previous year's purchases. If the customers bought more than last year, or ordered something different, then we had a problem. As Murphy would have it, such problems usually cropped up just as we were about to start production. The Production guys would yell at the buyer, who in turn yelled at the supplier, who worked overtime and used airfreight to get the materials to us. By this stage the order was inevitably late, so the customer would start yelling at the Sales Director, who would then yell at the Operations Director, as well as anyone else from the factory who was unfortunate enough to cross his path.

But that was just one of the facets of the problem. At Sellotape, there was no system for scheduling orders through the factory. In one of the plants, for example, the routine procedure was to run off a list of overdue orders and to pass these to the factory, where they were dealt with in whatever sequence best suited the operators. Therefore, orders would not in fact get to the factory floor until they went overdue. This meant that the only orders that were satisfied on time were those that could be met from stock.

Prior to my arrival, the role of the Operations Director had developed into one of 'Sello Superman'. When an important customer began shouting, Sales called for the Ops Director to save the day. Donning his superhero uniform, he would then leap into the fray, cutting through all the obstacles using his superhuman powers, as he personally shepherded this one particular customer's order through the factory and onto a truck. With the irate customer placated, the Sales Department would throw garlands at our superhero. Meantime, back at the factory, everything would have degenerated into chaos and disarray. All the other orders would have been delayed or simply put aside until a later date. The following day, another customer would ring in and treat someone else in Sales to a load of verbal abuse about his late order, and the same pantomime would begin all over again.

When I arrived it was assumed that I would don the garb of a new superhero. After all, that was what Ops Director did, so everyone believed. They were in for a rude shock. I explained that I had no intention of joining everyone else chasing rabbits down holes. If I too spent my life down rabbit holes, we would be lost forever. Someone had to stay above ground to direct the hunt, and that was my role. The reaction to this was one of undisguised disbelief. "But who will solve the problem when a customer phones up and wants to kill the Sales Director?" they asked.

With Sellotape, any supply problems were seen as the sole responsibility of Operations. The job of Sales was to get the orders in. Meeting those orders was Operations' problem. There was no joint responsibility for satisfying customers. Naturally, this provided a bullet-proof alibi for Sales when they missed the budget. "Give us the service and we will meet the budget" was the standard response when anyone queried why turnover was short of the target. While this might have contained an element of truth, it was used as a decoy to lure attention away from other problems in Sales.

Month-ends were the source of other crises. What counted was how much was recorded as dispatched by 5p.m. on the last day of the month. This is a widespread technique for propping up the sales and profit figures. Practically speaking, it meant the Ops Director shuttling between Sales Order Processing, the Warehouse and the Factory, plucking out orders to push out of the door. Meanwhile some poor clerk would be frantically entering the backlog of dispatch confirmations into the computer before the books were closed. The effect on the factory was devastating. Yet more chaos reigned while those last orders were unceremoniously rushed out, taking precedence over everything else.

The culture of the whole business was based on fire-fighting, with the heroes being those who were good at putting out fires. Order and control were sneered at and anyone advocating such wimpish action was ignored. Truth to tell, some of the managers got a real adrenaline rush out of fire-fighting and so had little or no motivation to find a better way. There is nothing quite like the buzz that comes from resolving a problem and all too many of us become addicted to it. The only good aspect of the culture was the focus on customers. There was a real awareness of the need to satisfy and indeed to delight customers, and this was the driving force behind everything that went on. But, somehow, this noble cause had turned into a misguided crusade. No matter what the customer expected or demanded, the business was turned upside down in an effort to meet it. To illustrate to people that the customer focus had got out of hand, when told yet again: "But the customer wants it", I finally found myself saying, "So, if the customer wants a second-hand bicycle, are we suddenly in the pre-owned bicycle business?"

The business was completely dominated by Sales. Operations was expected to respond to whatever Sales demanded – no matter what, no matter when. The result was an Operations function that could never succeed in satisfying Sales' requirements and their attempts to do so resulted only in confusion, frustration and very high cost.

The problem had its roots in a complete lack of appreciation, at top management level, of how to manage a supply chain, or even of any of the principles of supply chain management. In the absence of anything better, they had resorted to fire-fighting as the management tool of choice. Before we could tackle the problem, I had to convince the top management to learn about supply chain management. Getting senior managers to appreciate that there is something they might be able to learn is always difficult, particularly when they have been in the business for a long time. The attitude tends to be one of "We know this business and we don't need this. Our business is different from the others". I needed to get the senior management (the directors and heads of each function) together to teach them how a supply chain should be managed.

I started working on the MD of the time, but my persuasive powers got me nowhere. He wanted me to just go and fix the problem. Why did I need to tie up all the senior managers? After all, the customer service problem was the fault of Operations. The rest of them had to be out there looking after customers. Eventually, I gave him Ling and Goddard's book 'Orchestrating Success' to read. One night some weeks later, he was unable to sleep while away on a business trip. With the television being in a foreign language and nothing better to do, he read the book. It did the trick. He suddenly appreciated that the whole business had to be involved in meeting the needs of the customers. It was not just Operations' problem. I got my day with the senior managers.

I had learnt about supply chain management over the years, before I had ever heard mention of the term, when faced with developing processes to manage demand and supply in a number of businesses. I had eventually got into it in a big way when I worked for SmithKline Beecham. I had been asked to help sort out a supply problem in one of the business units and ended up developing a training course with the help of two colleagues. I planned to use this course as the basis of the training for Sellotape.

Before attempting to train the senior management group, I wanted them to reach an appreciation that they did in fact have a problem and that it was not just my problem. I needed to capture their attention – to earn the right to teach them. The best way to do this was by exposing them to an experience that revealed the problem in an unthreatening way. I had a 'supply chain game' up my sleeve that would do this.

The game goes something like this:

Six players are seated side by side, each at a small table separated from the adjacent ones by foot or so. Each player plays the role of one link in a supply chain:

- Factory ➔ ● Central Warehouse ➔ ● Area Warehouse ➔
- Depot ➔ ● Distributor ➔ ● Retailer

The product is Lego blocks, or anything similar. Each player must maintain specified minimum stock levels and observe minimum order quantities. They are not allowed to talk to one another, communicating only by passing orders written on a piece of paper. (This represents the reality of life in a business that has no supply chain management processes.) Customer orders are placed on the Retailer. To satisfy this demand, the Retailer orders stock from the Distributor and so on down the chain to the Factory. Each player keeps records of how much stock they hold and the back orders. To make the exercise more true to life, the Retailer is equipped with a whistle, which he is encouraged to blow loudly at the downstream chain every time he cannot meet a customer order because of lack of stock.

In this game, the customer demand remains relatively flat, starting at two units and rising to four. It then remains constant as the game progresses through ten rounds. What always happens across the supply chain is a rapid escalation in back orders at the Retailer end (accompanied by a lot of frantic whistle blowing), while at the same time stocks begin to accumulate in the middle of the chain. By the tenth round, the whole chain is completely out of balance with huge stocks in the middle, an idle 'Factory' and a frustrated 'Retailer' with an enormous pile of backorders.

The key learning point is that this represents the simplest of supply chains, with a single product, only six links in the chain and with everybody sitting in one room. One can imagine what happens when the participants are invited to consider the potential chaos in an actual supply chain, with scores of products and the individual links in the chain separated by sometimes hundreds of miles. At this point, most people tend to be sitting up and paying full attention.

The game is then repeated with two improvements:

- Each link is permitted to talk to his or her immediate neighbour in the chain. (In practice, one physically moves the tables closer to one another, making communication easier.)

- The Retailer publishes a forecast of future demand before each round for all in the chain to see.

With these refinements, everything goes much more smoothly. There is much less stock built up and lower backorders across the length of the chain. The lesson is clear: communication and forecasting makes the chain work. At this stage, all resistance vanishes and one can start the training.

When the top brass of Sellotape GB walked into the room and saw tables laid out with Lego blocks, they must have thought that the lunatic had finally been given the keys to the asylum. To their credit, they contained their scepticism and went along with me, but there were certainly some funny looks shot in my direction. As usual, the game worked its magic and I earned the right to be heard on the subject of supply chain management.

The course content included sections on forecasting and inventory management, as well as sales-and-operations planning and policies. Each section was followed by some task work in which the group worked on real problems in the business. By doing this, they were not only learning about supply chain management, they were also starting to build the foundations for the processes we would be using in the business. By the end of the day, we had two critical building blocks in place. We had agreed on the form and membership of regular Sales and Operations planning meetings and we had a list of the policies that needed to be developed.

The Sales and Operations planning (SOP) meetings were key to the whole exercise. (Fig 7.1)

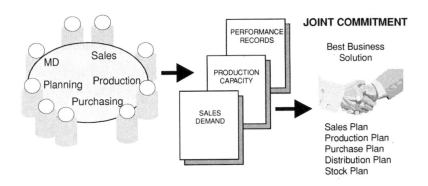

Fig 7.1 - Sales and operations planning

These were to be the forum in which Sales and the various functions in Operations would get together to sort out the supply problems that were dogging the business. The MD had to be involved in these, because compromise would be required from both sides in the interests of reaching the best solution for the Company. Compromise was inevitable. Production did not have infinite capacity; Purchasing could not supply material at a moment's notice and Sales could not sell just what suited production. Only the MD could make the decision as to where that balance should be struck in the best interests of the business as a whole.

The very first task for the SOP meeting was to develop a set of policies by which the business would manage the supply chain. There had to be a set of basic rules that everyone would agree upon and use to plan their activities. We could no longer work with disparate expectations in areas such as lead times, where Sales would often decide that a few days was appropriate, while production would tend to see things in terms of weeks. Other topics for which policies were desperately needed included stockholding, forecasting and minimum order quantities.

We tackled the policies one by one. Each time, we had a difficult and sometimes heated debate as compromises were hammered out. Finally, all the members of the SOP team were prepared to sign their names to the policy. While compromise meant there was a degree of dissatisfaction for everyone, at least there was agreement to abide by one rule, and everyone knew what this rule was, even if they didn't like it. Inevitably, because the business had been Sales orientated in the past, the result was that Sales were the 'losers' in this process, having to compromise more than anyone else. This left them with the feeling that Operations was 'taking over'. Indeed, we were trying to wrest a lot of control and power away from Sales, but only with the best of intentions. In the end, Sales would benefit by becoming the recipients of a reliable and competitive level of service for their customers. It was a painful process, but it was absolutely essential for deciding how we wanted the business to run. The degree of difficulty we had in reaching agreement was a reflection of the problems and conflict with which the business had been living for years. No wonder we could not get the goods out of the door on time.

One of the criticisms that was levelled at me on a few occasions was that we were creating something resembling a civil service bureaucracy, and I appreciate that it might indeed have appeared to be the case. I maintain, however, that to sort out the company, we needed to change the culture from 'fire-fighting' to 'reliable and effective'. To do this meant writing down the new rules of the game and making sure that everyone knew what rules were and played by them. Once this was the case, we could throw the book away. It is the same with most sports. They have strict and carefully documented rules known by all the players. But you don't see the rulebook in a match. Without these rules, matches would be anarchy. At Sellotape, the procedures meant we were creating a game in which we all knew what was going on. I was sure that once everyone knew the rules and played by them, we could dispense with the bureaucracy and focus on becoming good at playing the game.

We also built in a capability to allow for exceptions to the rules. Good business practice dictates that there will always be times when the rules have to be broken. The trick is to ensure that the reasons for breaking the rules represent genuine benefits for the business, and that they remain the exception. To ensure this, we set up procedures for managers to sign off exceptions, while we built an additional 10% spare capacity in the production plan to cope with panic orders. In this way we retained control while having sufficient flexibility to adapt to reasonable customer needs.

With the supply chain training day having been so successful, we rolled it out until everyone who was involved in the process was up to speed. What took the time was hammering out all the policies and then implementing them. For example, setting up a process for producing sales forecasts was particularly time consuming. A lot of people needed to be involved and trained, and a lot of data had to be collected and evaluated before we could start generating any kind of meaningful forecast. Meanwhile, the myriad smaller supply chain problems in the factories was being whittled away. The factory scheduling was overhauled, purchasing procedures revised, stock control improved and measurements put in place.

We even had to devise new procedures for picking the orders in our consumer warehouse. I remember being summoned to the head office of one of the high street retail chains to explain why our deliveries were constantly days late. When I explained that we actually had the products on the shelf of our warehouse, but our layout and procedures for picking and packing the orders were so inefficient that we could not get them onto the vehicles in time, they just could not believe their ears. It was a meeting I remember vividly – unfortunately!

Slowly but surely we improved our service levels. (Fig 7.2)

There were many false dawns and frustrations along the way, but we eventually got it right. Along the way, where it gave us an edge in the market, or where the market demanded it, we cut our lead times. The phones rang less often and the staff in Customer Service began to smile again. The air of crisis slowly became one of calm control, eventually being replaced by one of slick efficiency.

Management Stuff

Supply chain management is a critical element of any manufacturing business and in my experience most companies get it wrong. Computers cannot effectively manage the supply chain. They can grind the numbers and provide extremely useful information but they cannot take the decisions. These decisions, which rest upon compromise and balance, can only be made by people with knowledge of the business. All this has to be underpinned by good relationships between the people in the various departments. Such

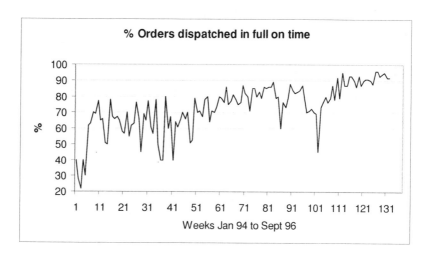

Fig 7.2 - Orders dispatch performance - foams plant

relationships can only develop where effective processes exist to facilitate good communication links among the parties in the supply chain.

Critical Success Factors

- Top management understanding of supply chain management principles.

- Top management involvement in managing the supply chain.

- Regular forums in which the supply and demand are compared and compromises developed until supply matches demand, both in the short and long term.

- A set of policies or rules agreed, accepted and observed by everyone in the business.

- A process for managing exceptions to the rules.

8

Using the ERP System to Support Change

'Systems' was one of the elements of our Vision. In hindsight, it would have been better to call this element something like 'Procedures', because 'Systems' implies computers. What we had in mind for the Vision went much further than just the use of computer systems. That said, the computer system supporting the business was going to be critical to us, if we were to build a world class operation.

The key to running a successful manufacturing business is having the right information made available to the people who can use it, at the time that they need it. 'Relevant, accurate, online information at the point of action,' as it said in our Vision.

When I started at Sellotape, I was impressed with the extent and use of the ERP system (or MRPII, as it was called in those days). When Franck and Rory bought the business, they had had to install a new system because of some potential conflicts of interests with other parties, the detail of which I never bothered to learn. The implementation had to be done in a hurry and so those areas that were considered critical to the business at the time, such as Finance and Sales Administration, received priority attention. Manufacturing systems had been included only to the extent that they were needed to support Sales and Finance. There had been no time to optimise the processes before automating them. Instead, there were an inordinate number of 'work-arounds', whereby the way in which the work was done or the data presented, had been adapted to suit the computer system. The result was that we had a semi-ERP system in use in the manufacturing areas. Unfortunately, rather than improving the situation in production, this actually made life more difficult.

The Ops management team had decided that the Critical Performance Area in the Systems element was 'operations information systems'. To improve these, we decided to do a full re-implementation of the ERP system in the Operations areas. We called it 'Project Quantum'.

I was fortunate to have Andrew Houston as a member of the Ops management team. He was one of the new boys recruited from outside, where he had already had hands-on experience of a similar project. He was to be the anchorman, providing the overall drive and guidance.

The strategy behind 'Project Quantum' was to let the users of the system develop the processes, so that they could design the system to meet their needs. The kind of system we wanted needed to be a tool for improving the way we worked. We refused point blank to have some box of wires and chips dictate how we mere mortals should work. It was going to be our system.

In order to move forward, we had to educate everyone who was to be involved in the project. They were to be trained in the basics of the system and how to apply it. It was on this basis that the Systems action plan was drawn up. (Appendix F)

When we came to write the plan, we were not exactly sure what we were letting ourselves in for. We did know, however, that it really was going to be a lot more complex than the plan suggested. But we felt we had no choice. Accurate information would be key to realising our Vision. There was no room for the kind of frustration that a lack of information can engender. On the positive side, this project represented a superb vehicle for empowering people to change their own ways of working. They would have the knowledge and information that would give them the means to change how the company worked. The project would also promote the individual's creative abilities in terms of finding better ways of doing things. This was completely aligned with our Vision of empowering people to bring about change, while improving their own performance and that of the business.

There were, however, a number of flies in the ointment. Firstly, the project would necessarily involve the whole Company, because we could not develop the Ops systems in isolation. It would therefore require the active participation of a lot of people across the business. Secondly, it was going to cost a substantial amount of money, largely to fund the high level of training. We therefore needed to have the whole executive management team on board. Having a powerful sponsor was also critical. This meant including an Executive training programme in the action plan that would ensure that the top management understood what the capabilities of the final system would be. Once they had grasped the potential benefits, we were sure of securing their approval.

Sure enough, in the very early stages of setting up the project, Rory queried whether this whole exercise would deliver the hard benefits that would justify the investment in time and money.

"We don't have any option," I replied. "We cannot continue to run the business with the system in its current state." I proceeded to elaborate on some of the problems. For example, the production plans were compiled from a mix of data from the main system, from paper inputs and from data transferred between computers using floppy disks. (Fig 8.1)

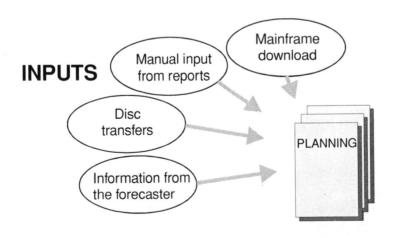

Fig 8.1 - The old production planning process

To generate the sales forecast, data was being processed through six stand-alone PCs, followed by two days of manual keying in of data, resulting in bad data being produced and unnecessarily last-minute demands on suppliers. As for the physical stock, this seldom even resembled what was on the books. This caused wild swings in the profits and a great deal of anguish. Just getting these crazy processes fixed would save money and improve business efficiency. Unfortunately, I could not put a monetary value on the benefits.

At that time, vendors of ERP systems tended to trot out very impressive figures representing savings in stock, increased productivity and improvements in numerous other areas – all of which implied that installing an ERP system (theirs, naturally) would represent a licence to print money. We had picked up this tune and played it for Rory, albeit with a touch of reserve. Though still somewhat sceptical, he gave us the go-ahead and agreed to be the project sponsor.

I was very pleased. Having him on board gave real weight to the project. But I was going to have to work hard to keep him on track. Every so often, he would call me in and demand to know when and where he was going to see the payback. He wanted to see benefits during the implementation, not just at the end. My protestations that the money would only appear some time after the new system went live left him unimpressed; but, despite his misgivings, he stuck with us.

The project team itself ended up with about 20 members, of which about five were full time. At some time or other, almost everyone in the business was involved to some degree, and it became a real driver of change. The results were significant. The accuracy of the base data improved dramatically, with bill-of-material accuracy rising to 98% and warehouse stock accurate enough to inspire the confidence that, when one went to collect an item, it would in fact be there. (Fig 8.2)

Customer Services staff could now see exactly where an order was in the factory, whereas previously they had not even been able to see the production plan. Purchasing processes were streamlined (Fig 8.3) and an integrated forecasting system replaced the six-PC process. (Fig 8.4)

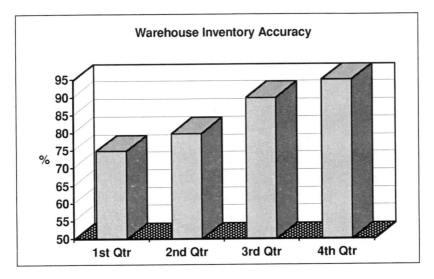

Fig 8.2 - Warehouse stock accuracy

PURCHASING

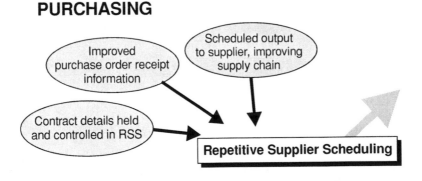

Fig 8.3 - New purchasing processes

We now had information to tell us how well we were doing on the factory floor. (Fig 8.5)

The readily available information on past and future requirements of materials and goods became a veritable armoury for the buyers, who used these new weapons to good effect, extracting vast savings and service benefits from suppliers over the next few years. This factor

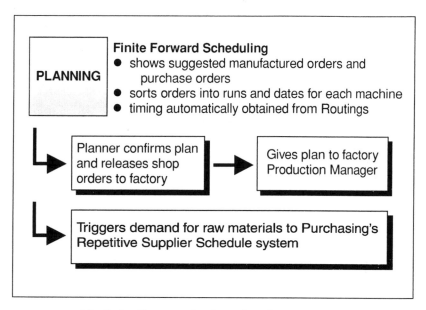

Fig 8.4 - New production planning processes

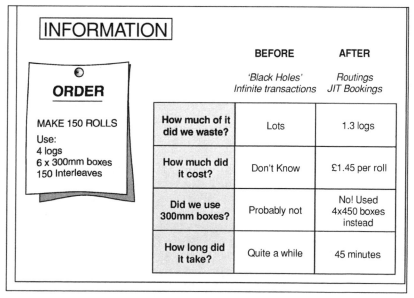

Fig 8.5 - New information

alone was to have a significant impact on the business profitability.

'Project Quantum' became an enabler of change, both during the implementation stage of the system and after the project went live. During the project, many people learnt what a business process was and how the old processes had worked. They then had the opportunity to design new and better ones – an exciting and rewarding prospect in itself. They were able to test their ideas, without any risk to themselves or to the business, by piloting them in a conference room setting before they were put into practice. Then, they were able to see the results of their work in real life. This was real empowerment.

The individuals and teams decided for themselves what new information they wanted and how it should be presented. At the end of the project, there was much more useful information available and a lot less useless data around to confuse matters. We had gone a long way towards meeting the aspiration in the Vision to have 'relevant accurate and online information at the point of action'.

To this day, Rory remains sceptical about the benefits of the project. It turned out to be almost impossible to put a finger on exactly what benefits were strictly attributable to Project Quantum. Rory argues that the business results that we achieved after Project Quantum could have been realised by just working smarter, and that we did not need the system to make these improvements. I completely disagree with this view.

Without the redesign of the processes and the new, easily accessible information, we could not have made the improvements in cost, inventory and customer service that we did. I also believe that the training of a wide range of people in the capability and use of the system empowered many of our employees to make improvements that we as management never got to hear about.

Rory and I have agreed to differ in our assessment of the benefits of ERP systems, but it does provide endless opportunities for us to have a friendly go at one another.

Management Stuff

An ERP implementation can be used as the core vehicle to drive a change programme in a business. In the Sellotape experience, while it was not the central core of the programme, a system re-implementation was fully integrated into the change programme and supported it in many ways.

Key Points

- The implementation was user driven rather than system driven.

- User training enabled people to utilise the system and adapt it to support their needs.

- The project was sponsored by the highest level in the business.

- The direct benefits from the ERP implementation proved difficult to quantify.

Part 2

Organisation Design

9

The Birth of Sellotape Industrial

The Vision programme was succeeding in changing the nature and performance of Sellotape GB Operations and the effect was beginning to spill over into the Company as a whole. Rory and Franck wanted to roll out the new culture and ways of working to the rest of the Sellotape Group. I was asked to take on responsibility for all of the Group manufacturing operations and invited to become a member of the Group Executive – the management board that steered the Group businesses as a whole. This gave me an insight into, and an opportunity to influence, the Group strategy and direction. The position – Group Executive Director: Operations and R&D – needed extra-large business cards just for the title!

After only some six months in this role, during which I made no significant impact on the business, a whole new direction emerged. The owners decided that, with the company now firmly in the black, it was time for them to realise their gains. Initially, this came as a bit of a shock to me, though in hindsight, it had always been on the cards. After all, neither Franck nor Rory had expressed a long-term view regarding Sellotape's future. They opened discussions with a variety of potential purchasers, but none of these was interested in buying both the consumer and industrial sides of the business as a whole. They all wanted either one or the other.

At the same time, although there had been a steady improvement over the previous few years, we were still unable to make the kind of breakthrough we had been looking for, in terms of significantly increasing the rate of improvement in profitability. We had made great strides forward.

● The Company as a whole was profitable.

- Nearly every country was profitable in its own right.
- Fixed Costs had been substantially reduced.
- Despatch performance was up to 95%
- Sales had been reorganised and focused
- Export markets had been revived
- Productivity had increased significantly
- Performance had improved throughout the entire Company.
- But, despite all this, the business was turning in only some 4% on sales, and it had begun to plateau at this level.

This was clearly not good enough, especially since the average return on sales in the industry was about 6% and our target was to get up to at least 10%. Furthermore, we were not prepared to be just another Tapes Company. We wanted Sellotape to be a high-class, high-profit, market leader. Below average, or even average, was unacceptable. With the newly found capability for improvement and the enthusiasm that was obvious in the workplaces, we knew that there was sufficient momentum to get us to the top.

Returning to the mediocre performance, we kept wondering how it was that we were stuck in this groove. What was it that was standing in the way? We took a step back and reviewed the situation. Two major obstacles seemed to be holding the business back, and the prospective buyers had latched onto the first of them. We were trying to run the consumer business and the industrial business as one. Secondly, while our individual functions were performing exceptionally well, they were operating separately, and not working in such a way as to maximise the benefit for the Company as a whole.

The market drivers for Sellotape's consumer side, as with most consumer businesses, were significantly different from those on the industrial side. Lead times were short; products were standard with little technological content; packaging was all-important and changed regularly, and short-term promotional activity was a key feature.

By contrast, in the industrial business, lead times were generally longer; many of the products were designed and manufactured specifically to customer specification; R&D was essential for new product development; packaging was purely functional, and the product had high technological content. All of these factors meant that the processes and people in the business supporting these two different markets needed to behave and respond differently.

At Sellotape, there was only one structure to support both the consumer and industrial sides. It had been installed in the early days, when the business was in trouble, as a way of reducing the overhead burden. I had no quarrel with that: drastic times need drastic solutions. But we were now entering a different era in the evolution of the Company. It was time to restructure the business, separating the consumer and industrial businesses so that they could prosper independently. I like to think that the structure we had developed in Operations, where we had separated the product and market streams, provided the inspiration for this revolution.

However, prising the two apart would not be easy, particularly in the UK. The Finance, Administration and IT functions supported both segments of the business, while within Operations, some of the disciplines (R&D, Quality Assurance and Project Engineering) had been set up to support the whole business. As Operations Director and champion of the Vision, I had, moreover, strongly promoted the idea that we were all in it together – as members of a single family. Besides the difficulties of getting this change of emphasis across to the shop floor without crushing everyone's sense of identity, I was also very conscious that, having worked so hard on getting the overheads down, by separating the businesses, we ran the risk of increasing them again. We could, therefore, end up with an even less profitable business.

I took on the task of designing the shape of the new industrial business. This meant identifying just where the problems were likely to appear and developing ways to overcome them. It was another challenge and I looked forward to spending a good part of my day devising a whole new business that would take the Sellotape revolution to the next level.

Nevertheless, I found myself on something of an emotional roller coaster during all this. I was enjoying the recognition that came with my new appointment to the Group Ops job and I was excited by the novelty of working on the design of the industrial business, but I still had that nagging uncertainty that goes with the prospect of a change in ownership. Who would buy us and when would it happen? And what would the new owners do with Sellotape? Would everyone's hard work have been merely to line the shareholders' pockets, or was there going to be anything left of value for the workforce and the Company as a whole? The issues kept going round and round in my head. It was speculation that was doing me no good. There was only one real way out and I took it. I resolved to get on with the job – just enjoying the new challenges and opportunities that had come my way. In the end, helping to make Sellotape a top-class company would be the best course of action for all of us.

My new responsibility meant taking my hand off the UK Operations' tiller and passing much of the control to my management team. I had no worries there, because they were all highly capable; but, for them, my rather sudden withdrawal from the day-to-day management caused some initial anxiety. Their champion was no longer to be seen holding the torch and driving progress. They felt the shift of emphasis deeply enough to express their concern to me.

"I know that I am not around a lot of the time and we have less time to talk to one another," I said, "but we are moving on to a new stage in the life of the Company and we shall all have to learn to adapt."

Nevertheless, I shared some of their emotion. The Ops team had gone through a lot together, experiencing all the phases of team development – forming, storming, norming and performing. What we were now experiencing was the mourning phase, where the original team was changing and the development process was starting afresh. Needless to say, the team re-formed in a slightly different shape, with the managers taking charge of their own destiny. They no longer needed my somewhat paternalistic, sometimes heavy hand on what they did. Without it, they blossomed.

In the new industrial business, we needed to get everyone working together for the good of the whole Company. The main problem was that there was a tendency for each manager to look after his own patch and this was definitely holding back the performance. I was probably more guilty of this than most. I, for one, was determined to run an efficient Operations function and nobody was going to get in the way. Sometimes, it has to be said, this was not perhaps in the best interests of the Group. For example, when it was a question of maximising the efficiency of manufacture, I would stubbornly insist that the rules and procedures be followed to the letter, even when it might have been better to turn a blind eye in order to help a customer out of a hole. This rather sad approach had been born out of a misguided sense of purpose – I had been charged with sorting out Operations and I was going to do it.

This insular approach also reared its head across national borders. With each country (Switzerland, Germany, France, Italy, Benelux, Scandinavia Canada and the UK) having a local MD, who jealously guarded his individual business regardless of the consequences for Sellotape as a whole, the difficulties were magnified considerably.

We needed a different kind of organisation – one designed around the business, rather than around geographical or cultural boundaries; which took a global approach to markets and the business; and which was focused on three segments: foams, sealant and tapes.

We decided to call the new business 'Sellotape Industrial'. It was simple and to the point. It retained the heritage of the Sellotape name and the values of reliability and consistency that the brand carried in the marketplace. At the same time, it described exactly what the Company did.

Our aim was to retain all the good things that we were doing, but to do things better by working together. From this desire grew the mission statement for the new business – 'Working together in better way'.

After some work and several false starts, Franck and Rory agreed to my proposed organisation structure, which I felt confident would allow us to build this new global business (Fig 9.1). Only one issue remained to be resolved. We needed an MD.

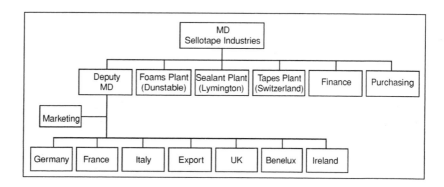

Fig 9.1 - The basic Sellotape Industrial organisation structure

I was offered the job. I resisted in much the same way that tradition dictates new Speakers must behave in the British Parliament. Even though they are only too eager to take up the post, they have to make a show of resisting the appointment and have to be wrestled into the chair.

Management Stuff

There are only two principles I want to highlight from this chapter:

- Business and organisation structures have to change as the business evolves in order to optimise performance.

- A high-performing team will suffer a temporary period of mourning on the loss of a member or a change in the nature of the leadership, but it will quickly re-form and continue to excel.

10

'Working Together in a Better Way'

Basking in the glow of my new status and cock-a-hoop about the fresh challenge of leading Sellotape Industrial to unprecedented levels of performance, I was nevertheless plagued with doubts about my ability to crack this problem. True, I had succeeded over the previous years, but this was going to be a much tougher matter. I could not do it all on my own. Only by harnessing the combined intellect and enthusiasm of every single manager, in what was to become my organisation, would I be able to pull it off.

'Working together in a better way' – our new mission statement – encapsulated the whole idea. Only by operating like this could we capitalise on all the talents and skills that we had across the business and create a really prosperous enterprise.

There was ample evidence from around the Company that we had a very capable group of managers working for us. What we needed was to find a way of channelling all this experience and energy in the same direction. This would ensure that we would make the new business into something to be really proud of. A multiplier effect was required. We had to keep all the good things that we had been doing in our functions and businesses, and then multiply the impact of these by working as a team, to share all the experience and learning. This would reveal those opportunities that had been falling between the cracks. It was these lost opportunities that were holding back our progress towards becoming a world-class performer in our industry. My task was to make the whole much greater than the sum of its component parts.

Naturally, after what we had been through, I was confident that the new organisational structure would provide the foundation for a new kind of business. But this was not enough. This structure merely dictated the lines of command and control. We needed the new organisation to have a whole new character.

I sat down to review the elements of what was needed:

- a unique culture, owned by the people and focused on performance
- common goals for everyone in the organisation
- effective cross-functional and cross-national relationships and teamwork
- maximum use of the existing skills and talents within the organisation
- a profit orientated business.

This last point would be, I knew, somewhat contentious. When we had discussed Sellotape's primary purpose amongst the managers, there had been some heated debate. Many believed that the company existed to serve the customer, with profits being a secondary issue, coming as a natural consequence of having the customer as the prime focus. Others worked on the premise that the business existed to make a profit and looking after customers was the way to achieve this result. Though not a dirty word, the term 'profitability' was the source of some considerable embarrassment. We tended to fight shy of mentioning 'it' to the outside world in general and certainly not to our customers. The argument went: "After all, if the customer knows we are making a profit, they will want lower prices." Somehow one side of the debate had, in my view, lost sight of the fact that no customer wants to deal with an unprofitable business. Depending on a marginally profitable supplier could be potentially dangerous for a customer and might ultimately expose him to the risk of a sudden collapse of part of his supply chain.

We needed to shift the paradigm from embarrassment to pride. In the new organisation, we wanted profit to be the focus of our efforts. In addition, we wanted to be in a position where customers wanted to do business with us precisely because we were successful in every respect.

To create this new character and get the whole organisation working as a highly tuned team, we needed to tackle all the factors that influence team performance. (Fig. 10.1)

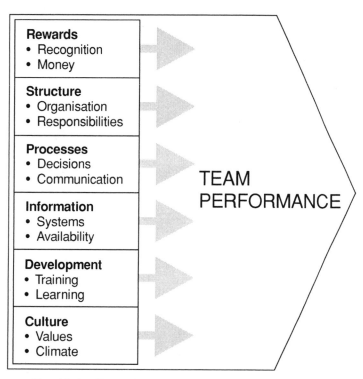

Fig 10.1 - Factors influencing team performance

In fact, what we actually wanted was a number of teams within the Company, all operating in concert with one another. To start with, we needed a team to lead the business: a Board who would take the major business decisions.

I am a great believer in small teams and I felt this Board should not exceed six members. With Franck and Rory as non-executive Directors, the finance director, myself as MD, together with the deputy MD, we had a nearly full house. What was missing was representation from the people at the sharp end of the business where the money would actually be made. This posed a problem. How could we keep a small, tightly knit Board, while at the same time involving a wider group of the managers in the running of the business? A really creative solution was needed. The solution came to me one night in the bath. Just what prompted the new idea is open to speculation, but

I was certain it would work. We would have a Senior Management Team and Board that overlapped one another. (Fig. 10.2)

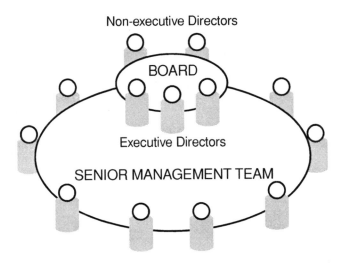

Fig 10.2 - The Senior Management Team and the Board

The three executive directors would be members of both the Board and the Senior Management Team. The rest of the Senior Management Team would be made up of managers who were responsible for a large segment of the business, or individuals who could bring some significant value to the team. Clearly, the formal structural logic for whom should be on the Senior Management Team needed to be dumped if we wanted to run the business with forums and groups that allowed people to exercise their individual talents. It was a radical departure for us and begged the question: "So who does what in all this?"

The first thing to sort out was the role of the non-executive directors and, more importantly, what they were NOT going to do. I was concerned that Franck and Rory, having been in control for so long, would have some difficulty taking their hands off the wheel. But winning their acceptance was essential if we were to succeed in creating an organisation with the new character that we all agreed we needed. They would have to back off and let us run the show. In the future, if Franck was genuine about wanting something done in the business, he would have to work with the new teams. I drew up a set of rules of engagement:

Non-execs are not:

- to get involved in running the day-to-day business
- to initiate any projects without the approval of the Board
- to attempt to manage people who did not report to them
- to change priorities without the agreement of the M.D.

I presented these to Franck and Rory and was met by only token resistance. To give them their due, in all the ensuing change process, I only had to pull out the document once to remind them to behave themselves.

Having won this first battle, I set to work on helping to clarify the roles of the Senior Management Team and the Board. We needed to set out what each was to do in leading the business. The roles of the two groups were to be distinct from one another, and each group had to be absolutely clear about what the purpose of the other was and to stick to their own knitting. An overlap of membership didn't mean an overlap in the roles and responsibilities of the teams. In fact, when we thought about it, the roles divided out very neatly:

The Board was there to:

'Ensure delivery of Company performance'

This meant:

- defining the direction and strategy
- developing the Company's business plan
- setting Company objectives
- allocating resources
- establishing Company policy
- managing the overall performance
- approving capital expenditure.

The Senior Management Team represented:

'The Soul of the Company and the owners of the Culture'

Their job was:

- executing policy
- developing and sponsoring the Company vision
- communicating within the Company and to the organisation as a whole
- co-ordinating activity across the Company
- controlling Company projects.

Once these teams were in place with their defined roles, we would have bodies that would manage the operation of the business; be responsible for the culture; create the vision; and lead the business toward this Vision.

In addition, we also needed to transform ourselves to be able to deliver the kinds of performance levels we had set our sights on. This would involve changing the way we approached the markets, the processes we used and what people did. We needed a further refinement; another window through which to look at the business – one that would allow us to see differently what we were and what we did, that would inspire us to find new ways of achieving the multiplier effect.

I struggled with this one. My background in manufacturing kept getting in the way. I was stuck in my own little paradigm and kept on coming up with teams based around the factories. My mind-set would not stretch that little bit further to be really creative. Fortunately, Jacques Tencé, my partner and Deputy MD came up with the answer.

Jacques had spent a few years working primarily as a marketing consultant for the Sellotape Group, before joining the company fully when we started setting up the industrial business. But even then, as a wage slave, he only worked for us three days a week. The rest of the time he devoted to studying to be a psychologist – something that allowed him much more scope than that of just being a manager and director. He was our resident shrink, coach and conflict resolution expert. It was a role that turned out to have inestimable value.

Whenever personal relationships interfered with business, or someone had a personal problem, Jacques would invite them out to dinner, get inside their heads and help them to solve their problem. All the managers accepted him in his two very different functions: as the deputy MD, he was the boss and provided clear direction to the selling and marketing activities; but, when he was the amateur psychologist, he was a friend and confidante to anyone who needed him. He also kept me on track, guiding me away from my tendency toward authoritarianism whenever I was under pressure. He always encouraged me to break out of my preferred operational mode of relying purely on logic to consider instead how things felt – something that does not come naturally to me. Without his contribution, Sellotape Industrial would never have achieved the results it did.

Jacques' idea for a vehicle to transform the business was to have teams built around the three product technologies; tapes, sealant and foams. The teams would:

- be cross-functional
- include representatives from the major geographic markets, wherever they were
- manage their sector across the whole Company
- look beyond the day-to-day.

Their prime objective would be to deliver a step-change in financial performance. Their scope of activities covered the supply chain, from supplier to end customer, all markets and all countries. They would work on a matrix basis, integrating with the line functions.

We decided to call these groups 'Business Teams'. (Fig. 10.3)

This arrangement marked a significant shift in direction. It would bring together people who had never worked with one another to deal with issues that were both new and of definite interest to them. For example, the MD of Sellotape Germany, who sold a great deal of sealant in his market, would be a member of the Sealant Business Team. This would give him an opportunity to influence the development and manufacture of sealant in a way that had never been possible in the past. Furthermore, because some team members would effectively be 'outsiders', with new and unfettered ideas, they would be able to think the unthinkable – something which those involved in the day-to-day operations would be unlikely to do. This ran the risk that much of the 'unthinkable' would be complete rubbish; but, if just one or two of these off-the-wall ideas worked, it could transform the whole business.

This new way of looking at the business also gave us an opportunity

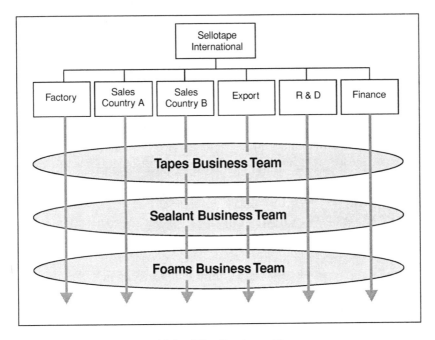

Fig 10.3 - The Business Teams

to focus our R&D more effectively. With an R&D lab at each of our three factories, we deemed it eminently sensible to have each one focus on a single product segment, rather than each of them attempting to be expert at everything. Each R&D department was to be allied with one Business Team, which would give the team the capability to develop its own technologies and try new things, while simultaneously creating centres of technical excellence for the Company.

The Board would appoint the Business Team leaders, but would not get involved in the choice of who were members of the teams. This was up to the team leaders to decide. We resolved only get involved if a team started to become too parochial, or if, from our wider perspective, the functional or geographic balance looked wrong.

However, the business had no experience of any kind of matrix management and everyone thought of themselves as having one 'job' and only one 'boss'. As a result, the first problem that reared its head was how to explain the role of the Business Team Leader and how this would dovetail into existing line responsibilities. We needed some clever way of explaining a totally new concept by which individual roles and responsibilities changed, depending on the task in hand. Something simple was required that would explain this new working mode to everyone in the business. We were looking for something visual that could be easily translated into the various other languages in the Group. The idea presented itself of Business Team leaders wearing two hats to explain their dual roles. (Fig. 10.4)

Business Team Leader	Line Manager
• Cross-functional responsibility • Focus on one sector • No national boundaries • Leads cross-functional Team • Delivers step-change in the business sector	• Functional responsibility • Focus on function • Functional boundaries • Leader of his function • Delivers function performance

Fig 10.4 - The "two hat" model for Business Team Leaders

The manager would metaphorically don whatever hat signified the role he was currently playing. Each hat had a set of responsibilities associated with it, and employees were to expect him to behave differently, depending on which hat he was wearing at the time. As for the manager himself, he would have to adopt a different mentality and a different frame of reference, depending on the hat being worn.

A second area that was also going to pose particular problems was territory. With Business Teams, line managers and country managers all potentially working on the same issues, albeit from different perspectives, there was a risk of armed skirmishes breaking out at any time. It was a potential minefield. We had to define exactly who was going to be accountable for what and how the functions would cope with interventions from the Business Teams. Sorting this out would be key. If we did not succeed here, nobody would consider himself or herself accountable; decisions would not be taken, and the Business would melt down. The various teams would have to see themselves as part of the whole, working together in the overall best interest of the business. We drew up a simple guideline to answer these questions (Fig. 10.5), but we knew that it would only work on the ground if we had genuine teamwork, a shared culture and set of values, and everyone focused on one common goal.

Line Management *Achieve Unit Budget*	**Business Teams** *Manage Business Step-change*
• Day-to-day management of business performance • Meeting monthly/annual target • Time frame: 1 to 12 months	• Strategic and directional focus across all functions • Step-change in performance • Time frame: 3 to 24 months

Fig 10.5 - The roles of Business Teams and line management

All three Business Team leaders were members of the Senior Management Team; so it made sense to use this body to co-ordinate the activities of the three Business Teams. By reporting back on progress and ideas, the Business Team leaders would learn from one another, while the Senior Management Team could guide them collectively to focus on what was important to the Company.

However, meetings don't come without a price, and the logistics and cost of all these team get-togethers was a source of genuine worry. We didn't want the additional gains spent on precisely the process that was designed to make these gains happen. But that the meetings had to take place was a given. We were not about to create virtual teams. Moreover, we wanted the members of the teams to develop personal as well as professional relationships with one another – the kind of relationships that only come from spending time together, both in social and working situations. We wanted them to have dinner together the evening before a meeting and to develop that sense of camaraderie that seems only to develop from sharing bottles of wine.

Stage one involved drawing up a matrix detailing who would meet and at what frequency. The scenario was an absolute nightmare! Enormous amounts of time would be spent in meetings all over the world, with the main beneficiaries being the airlines. But, when a nettle has to be grasped, you just have to grin and bear the stings. If we wanted to create a truly global business, then there was no real alternative. We did resolve, however, that if it actually turned out to be a problem, we would just have to find some other way. It would not have been the first time we had tried something and got it wrong. (In fact, it all worked very well in practice. The various teams co-ordinated their meetings effectively, limiting both the travel time and cost, while the value that most people got from coming to the meetings far exceeded the cost in terms of money, time and effort.)

Most of this design work was done on the quiet by a very small team. Although we wanted to involve as many people as possible in designing the future for the new Company, we felt that, before we could announce the creation of Sellotape Industrial and our ambitious targets, we needed to have some idea about the overall implications and shape of the future. We were developing the outline of the picture. The team would have the opportunity to paint in the colours.

After some three months of design and planning, we were ready. We opted to announce the creation of the new Sellotape organisation at a Group management conference. I remember driving to the event and musing to myself about what a great time I had had being involved in such stimulating and interesting exercise. Then the realisation hit me: "Oh shit! Next Monday the whole bundle will fall in my lap and I will be responsible for making it all work!" I nearly crashed the car.

At the Group conference, the sound of a pin dropping would have come as a merciful relief. Everyone sat there in stunned silence. The look on the faces seated around the room said it all: "Not only have the lunatics taken over the asylum, they have appointed as MD that unco-operative despot of an Operations Director who has never seen a customer in his life!"

To many, it looked like the ultimate defeat. Operations had finally triumphed and taken over the business. Rules and procedures would be the rigorous norm, to be applied not only in Operations but also to Sales, customers and markets. Sellotape Industrial would turn into an unresponsive bureaucracy that would be insensitive to customers and their needs.

I am sure that a lot of futures were being pondered in those few moments. I was going to have to work hard to prove that I was not just an empire-building, overgrown Production Manager; that we actually were going to be working together in a better way.

Management Stuff

The division of the Sellotape Group into separate consumer and industrial businesses provided an opportunity to integrate previously independent units and functions into a single global entity. In doing this, a variety of cross-functional and cross-border working groups were needed to facilitate teamwork and communication. At the same time, the shareholders, who had previously held the senior executive management posts, delegated their executive responsibilities to the management.

Key Points:

- Teams were built around tasks and business activity.

- Team members were selected, not because of their job function or status in the hierarchy, but for their ability and potential to contribute to the purpose.

- Teams membership reflected the national diversity of the business.

- Each team had a very clearly defined role and the distinction between the roles of the teams was magnified.

- Where individuals had dual roles in the matrix, these were spelled out so that they were understood by everyone in the business.

- Responsibility for managing the daily business was separated from that of facilitating step change.

- Relative 'outsiders' were included in the teams to challenge the status quo, because they would not be bound by the old 'baggage of experience'.

- The shareholders gave management freedom to run the business, within the bounds of agreed performance expectations.

- Cross-national teamwork had an associated cost, but it was essential that this be funded in order to optimise teamwork and business performance.

11

A New Kind of Vision

We trained hard. But it seemed that every time we were beginning to
form into teams, we would be reorganised. I was to learn later in life
that we tend to meet any new situation by reorganising. And what a
wonderful method it can be for creating the illusion of progress while
producing confusion, inefficiency and demoralisation.

Gaius Petronius Arbiter
The Satyricon, First century, AD

The change we had announced represented the biggest shift in
direction in the whole history of the Sellotape Group and, together
with it, came a raft of apparently wacky ideas about how we were
going to run the new Company. The effect on the organisation was
like that of a bombshell. Most people were reeling and some were in
virtual shock. We needed to move quickly to halt the likely collapse
in morale and regain the confidence and commitment of everyone
across this somewhat diffuse business. We had to be proactive and
develop a new and compelling Vision as a framework within which to
make all the changes. Without such a framework, Sellotape would
descend into confusion, inefficiency and demoralisation.

It was a daunting path to take, but the success of the business
depended on the change and so we had to make it happen.
Fortunately, we had had the previous years of experience to help point
the way forward. The Senior Management Team's role was to be the
'owners of the culture and the soul of the business' and, although
there had not been enough time to develop a sense of team spirit or a
sense of identity, it was from here that the lead had to come. We started
the process afresh – developing the new Vision at another of those off-

site workshops. It seemed to me that, if we were smart, in addition to creating the Vision, we would also be able to use the workshop to get the Team through the 'forming' and 'storming' stages of team development, into 'norming' and well on the way toward the 'performing' phase.

However, pulling this group together into a cohesive and effective team was going to be far harder than it had been with the Ops team back in the old days of Sellotape GB. For a start, the Senior Management Team was bigger, with a mix of nationalities and functional backgrounds. Besides this, there was also a lot of personal animosity that had built up, over time, between individuals from different parts of the business. The Sales guys, for example, hated the Manufacturing chaps for having taken a large degree of control away from them, while the Germans distrusted everyone in the UK, because they had been let down so often. The Swiss, for their part, thought this was just another ploy to disguise an intention to close their factory. On top of all this, there were some very personal needles between a few individuals, resulting from a lack of knowledge and appreciation of one another's differing personal values, attributes and skills.

If we were to succeed in getting the Senior Management Team to be the champions of change across this widely distributed organisation, we would have to break down all these barriers and get the team working together. Some veritable magic, or at the very least some exceptionally nifty footwork, was going to be required to get each member of the team committed to the process and the team as a whole thinking with one mind.

It was time to bring in reinforcements. Overcoming my reluctance to involve outsiders, I rang Octave Consulting and invited John Taylor to come and play some of his management games at the workshop. I was looking for the sort of thing where six grown men balance on a narrow plank of wood, clutching tightly onto one another to avoid falling into an imaginary shark infested pool below them. I had favoured these kinds of games for years, because, while it is all seems a bit silly on the face of it, they are very effective at breaking down barriers and helping to build team spirit. John leapt at the chance to come along with a set of appropriate games, but suggested taking the exercise one step further. "Have you heard of the Herrmann Brain Dominance Instrument?" he asked. I looked mystified. "Whose brain damage instrument?" I responded.

John proceeded to enlighten me. "A scientist called Ned Herrmann has developed the left brain – right brain concept a stage further, defining four thinking styles," he said. "Herrmann represents these four styles as quadrants of a circle in The Whole Brain Model." (Fig 11.1)[1]

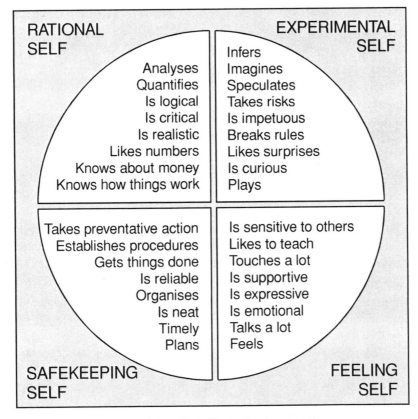

RATIONAL SELF	EXPERIMENTAL SELF
Analyses Quantifies Is logical Is critical Is realistic Likes numbers Knows about money Knows how things work	Infers Imagines Speculates Takes risks Is impetuous Breaks rules Likes surprises Is curious Plays
Takes preventative action Establishes procedures Gets things done Is reliable Organises Is neat Timely Plans	Is sensitive to others Likes to teach Touches a lot Is supportive Is expressive Is emotional Talks a lot Feels
SAFEKEEPING SELF	FEELING SELF

Fig 11.1 - The Whole Brain model

"According to Herrmann," John explained, "we tend to operate with a different level of preference for each of the four thinking modes, which influences our individual styles of thinking."

---

[1] *The Whole Brain Business Book* by Ned Herrmann, 1996. Published by McGraw-Hill. Reproduced with permission of The McGraw-Hill Companies.

John's view was that, by knowing our own dominant thinking style, as well as those of our colleagues, we would be able to understand one another better. This would result in our appreciating one another's values and why we tended to behave and think differently. John maintained that his games would illustrate our different individual thinking styles, and he emphasised the value of this for when we returned to the workplace. It would therefore provide exactly the kind of fast-track outcome I was looking for. The technique, he suggested, could then also be applied to assess the thinking style of the team as a whole, as if it were a single person. This sounded particularly interesting. If he was right, it would identify where the team's strengths lay and which styles we were lacking, and allow us to harness the power of all four thinking styles. This would help us to become much more effective and productive.

John knew all the right buttons to press. He was aware of my view that a sure-fire way to capture people's attention was to give them an opportunity to learn about themselves, and he knew that I had used something similar to help pull teams together in the past. His was a much more elegant instrument than those I had used and I felt sure that it would help us resolve the internal stresses in the team. It would be very useful to know any bias of thinking style we might have, both as individuals and as a group. By being aware of the kinds of things that we as a team would tend to miss or ignore, we could make a conscious and deliberate effort to adopt these other styles when considering how to solve problems. This, I reckoned, would enrich the quality of our thinking and decision-making and should bring some serious results.

But John had another trick up his sleeve. His sales patter was flawless. "Why not use the model to help you build your Vision for the Company?" he asked. "Each of the four quadrants could be adapted to describe one particular aspect of the Vision. For example, your profit and other performance targets would fit well in the 'Rational' quadrant, while how you want the company to relate to people naturally belongs in the 'Feeling' quadrant." He paused for a moment to see if I was taking the bait. Sensing my interest, he continued. "Under the 'Safekeeping' quadrant, you can describe the processes you want for managing the internals of the business and satisfying the customers." I was hooked. "And the creativity that you are looking for to break out of your current paradigm seems to be completely consistent with the concepts in the 'Experimental' quadrant". He just reeled me in.

This was the solution I was looking for. I wanted to avoid any resistance to the concept of building a vision. The history of the Operations Vision was well known and it was important that the Sellotape Industrial process be perceived as something fresh. If there was any hint that this was a carry-over from Operations, it would reinforce the impression that Ops was taking over the business. Something new was required. By using the Whole Brain Model, we could build both personal and team thinking styles into the Company Vision. This would go a long way toward making people feel more comfortable with the idea. It all looked like a very elegant solution and I took a gamble that it would work.

Time has the effect of resolving problems when change is in the air and some two weeks after announcement of the creation of the new organisation, the shock waves were beginning to subside. Work was proceeding on separating the business legally and organisationally and the work force, having accepted that the new direction might in fact have some merit, wanted to get started.

To create Sellotape Industrial, we had to split the engineering function in the UK, allocating people who had been serving both Consumer and Industrial to one or other business. One morning, I received a phone call from Richard Symes and Ian Stringer, the managers tasked with working out how to make it happen.

"It is just not possible to do this," they said. "We'll just have to keep one central engineering department and find some way of allocating the cost to the two businesses."

"No way!" I replied. There had to be a better solution.

"We need to meet and discuss it," said Richard, with a tone that implied he thought I was digging my heels in. I readily agreed to meet; but because of my travel schedule and a variety of other commitments, the first time we could get together was about ten days later. I steeled myself for a punch-up. We needed to split the two businesses and there had to be a way. I blotted out a two-hour time slot in my diary. In the event, the meeting lasted all of ten minutes.

Richard and Ian had found a way and it looked very promising.

The two-day Senior Management Team workshop was to take place at another scruffy hotel in the country. (Once again I wasn't going to provoke any adverse comments about wasting money.) It was to include 'hard' business debate, 'soft' personal sessions and some time for informal discussions – together with appropriate lubricant, of course. The warm-up exercises and introductions that we used in the Ops events were dispensed with. We were all keen to get stuck into the issues. No easing-in processes were required.

First on the list came the business imperatives. Our review of what we had achieved looked and sounded pretty good. We had a profitable business, turning in 4% return on sales, with a low fixed cost base and a revitalised sales force; customer service was up at 95% and we were moving from being a commodity producer to becoming a niche player. It would have been all too easy to sit back and pat ourselves on the back.

However, when we examined the targets we were expected to achieve, it was clear that this was not the time to be taking it easy. Our shareholders were looking for at least 10% return on sales. The normal reaction this kind of target would be: "That's impossible – the industry average is only 6%." Knowing that I would have to counter a response of this kind, I had sought out some relevant benchmarking data. There were no visits or videos featuring examples of company transformations this time, just a few pages from a brochure I happened to have picked up, published I think by the UK Department of Trade and Industry.

One particular manufacturer of domestic cookers had grown from £17m to £42m, despite a 30% decline in the market over the same period. How? By increasing its speed to market ten-fold and reducing its tooling costs by a factor of ten. Then, there was a carpet manufacturer that had increased productivity by 65% and reduced quality costs by half in one year. In all, I put up four similar examples, and then used two slides to present the team with the challenge. (Figs 11.2 and 11.3)

I worked hard at it, but still the team remained unconvinced. At least they had been prepared to give me a hearing. It was time to let John Taylor loose on them to introduce the Whole Brain Model.

Our current performance is not sustainable

- Most industry is undergoing this kind of transformation today.

- Today's innovation will be tomorrow's commodity.

- Quality is no longer a competitive advantage. It is the price of entry.

- Companies in our industry are consolidating.

- The price of commodities will continue to fall.

- More companies are focusing on providing customer specific product.

Fig 11.2 - The challenge to the Senior Management Team - Slide 1

We must transform ourselves to survive

- Sellotape Industrial must become a 12% EBIT* business to survive.

- We must achieve 8% EBIT in 1997.

- This means transforming ourselves into a new kind of organisation.

- If we don't, another management team will.

The transformation must begin now

Fig 11.3 - The challenge to the Senior Management Team - Slide 2
* EBIT - Earnings before Interest and Tax

Prior to the workshop, we had all completed a Herrmann Institute questionnaire and sent it off for evaluation. It was now for John to explain the concepts behind the instrument, the four quadrants and the meaning of our personal scores. The effect was electrifying. It was written on everyone's face. "Bloody hell!" we all seemed to be saying, "That's virtually spot on. How the heck can such a simple questionnaire get these results?" How indeed? But the results were there for all to see.

John allocated each thinking style a colour – blue for Rational, yellow for Experimental, red for Feeling and green for Safekeeping – and he handed out coloured caps to each of us indicating our individual preferred thinking styles. This was a fun and effective way of sharing our styles with one another and having this information on display all the time, so that we could observe one another's behaviour throughout the workshop. By the end of the two days, we would all come to know a lot more about the other team members and ourselves.

In the team, there was a rich mixture of thinking styles, but the blue caps were in a clear majority, suggesting that we had a strong rational bias. By contrast, red caps were a rarity amongst us. We were sadly short of individuals who preferred to think about the people, social and communication aspects of the business. One of our more perceptive colleagues quickly got to the root of the problem.

"So here we all are, being great at thinking up some very creative ideas and quantifying them precisely. Unfortunately, we are just bloody useless at turning these into something real in the business," he said, to peals of laughter. He was dead right. There was a decided deficiency in terms of our combined thinking styles and, when we looked back over the recent past, we could now clearly see why we had failed to breathe life into some of our bright ideas. This had brought about much frustration among those now wearing the blue and yellow caps. Finally, the blue caps started to understand that there was indeed a need for the red hats in a business and that such people were not just 'weak-kneed Willies', as they had previously thought. And perhaps those daydreamers with the yellow caps might actually come up with some novel ideas to revolutionise the business after all.

For our team, the idea of using caps as a metaphor for thinking style was a revelation, and we continued it for the life of the team. At our regular meetings, we would designate 'cap wearers' – one for each of the four colours. The role of the 'cap wearer' was to make a conscious effort to adopt the thinking style associated with the colour of his cap and to ask appropriate questions. This proved particularly useful in overcoming our lack of resource in the people and communication area. Furthermore, it helped us to develop as individuals, too. We soon found that we could all easily adapt our thinking style to take account of the social and personal aspects of business, if we made a conscious decision to do so. Indeed, we discovered some latent red cap talent in the team.

Our Finance Director, Ian McGillivray, was a classic 'blue', being a genius with facts and figures and, on the surface at least, not particularly interested in people. However, he soon revealed that he did in fact have excellent communication skills, to such an extent that, whenever I had to prepare a presentation or a communiqué, I would always ask Ian to go through what I had done and improve upon my efforts. He was also very skilled at presenting the monthly financials to the Senior Management Team, which he did in such a way that we all understood exactly what had happened and why. He would also skilfully clarify the issues and explain in very clear and simple terms what had to be done to improve the following month's results.

Back at the workshop, we got stuck into the 'silly' games in the garden. Besides helping reinforce our grasp of the Herrmann model and its relevance for us, the games went a long way towards easing the tensions between the team members. After all, it is difficult to stand aloof from a fellow team-mate after he has physically picked you up and posted you through a hole in a net strung between two trees in the garden of a hotel. Furthermore, that afternoon spent running around in the fresh air marked such a contrast to the intellectual challenges of the meeting room that we all felt hugely different when we returned to discuss the 'hard' business matters.

Having established the correct team dynamics, we could move on to developing the Vision, starting with a review of the current state of the business and a SWOT analysis. This went well because everyone felt secure enough to express their own views honestly, and thus had no need to hijack the discussion and launch into a personal crusade. Built into the exercise was an implicit element of 'letting off steam', since, in answering the question 'Where are we now?' we inevitably talked about the problems and frustrations that were holding us back. Having got all of this out into the open, we were ready to talk about the nature of the business we wanted to create. Once again, I resorted to Joel Barker and his same old 'Business of Paradigms' video. Only two of the team had seen the video previously and, as before, it proved a useful introduction to the visioning session, with Mr Barker succeeding in getting the team to open their collective minds to, at least, considering the unthinkable.

At this point, I must confess to having introduced a shortcut into the process. We did not have the luxury of spending two days chewing over every word of a vision statement. Nor was there time to reflect on how to present the vision, or the metaphor. I took the risk of drafting a vision as an 'Aunt Sally', which the Team would have the freedom to change in any way they saw fit. Much to my relief, the gamble paid off and within two hours we had succeeded in agreeing a Vision for Sellotape Industrial. (Fig 11.4)

Unlike with Sellotape GB, where a complete cultural turn around had been required, we had no intention of mounting a roadshow to preach this Vision throughout the whole organisation. The culture only needed a bit of a nudge to move it in the direction that we wanted it to go. By this stage, Sellotape had evolved into an organisation that could easily and speedily adapt to changes. We were not faced with the sort of history and intransigence that had pervaded the Operations function at the time I had joined the organisation. Those who could not, or would not, adapt quickly to changes had long since fallen by the wayside. Instead, there was a real appreciation throughout the company of the value of being able to adapt quickly to new circumstances. We now had a group of highly capable and motivated people who desperately wanted the business to succeed. All theyneeded was a clear direction and the removal of obstacles that were preventing them from doing their best. This was the aim of the Vision. It did not need to be sold. It was to be an effective tool that the workforce was keen to grasp. They would accept it without demur. They did not need convincing of its value.

There was, moreover, another underlying reason why I chose a low-key roll out of the Vision. The Sword of Damocles still loomed large. At some time in the foreseeable future, we would be sold. I believed it would have been both dishonest and misleading to create a lot of razzmatazz about a three-year vision, knowing full well that new owners, whoever they might be, could well want something different for their new acquisition.

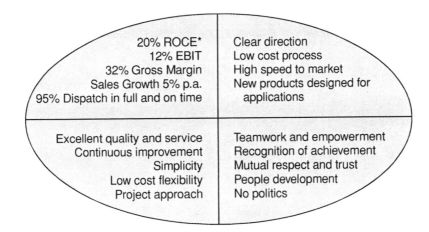

Fig 11.4 - The Sellotape Industrial Vision
*ROCE - Return on capital employed

Arriving at a Vision so early in the workshop was great on one hand. Unfortunately, neither John nor I had expected such rapid results and we were both caught somewhat flat-footed, with our preparation for the work sessions that were to follow not being ready when we needed them. This offended my desire for everything to be slick and professional, with the result that I took my frustration out on John, accusing him of not organising his work properly. As for the team, they were not fazed in the least, hardly noticing the desperate scramble that was going on behind the scenes. We finished off the workshop by drawing up and agreeing detailed action plans for establishing the new teams and communicating the Vision.

Everything had, in fact, gone better than we could have hoped, but, once again, I felt the need to get some sense of how determined we were as a team, to leap this incredibly high hurdle.

At the close of the workshop, I tasked John to conduct a confidential assessment of who believed it was indeed possible to make Sellotape into a business with the character and performance levels we had set out in the Vision. This was a serious matter and the team treated it as such, taking some time to examine their own inner thoughts and feelings before committing their answers to paper. We collected the responses and I asked John to count up the scores, so that there would be no chance of my reading the handwriting to find out who had voted which way. While John totted up the votes, I sat there feeling not the slightest apprehension or concern. I felt only a sense of quiet confidence that the team had accepted the challenge both intellectually and emotionally.

Nine of the ten members of the Team said they believed that we could do it. The tenth said that he was half convinced we could.

Management Stuff

The Herrmann Brain Dominance Instrument provided a core around which team members could build understanding and respect for one another in the Senior Management Team and it laid the basis upon which to establish team values and behaviours, the Company Culture and Vision.

The fact that people were ready for change made it possible for us to develop a shared vision in a very short time.

Key Points:

- Some kind of process was necessary to mobilise the organisation very soon after the announcement of the separation of Sellotape Industrial from the Consumer business.

- Employing an outsider to introduce a new tool into the process avoided cynicism about the process of establishing a Vision.

- Linking personal thinking style through team style to company vision secured rapid commitment to the Vision.

- The 'thinking-styles' exercise was carried through from the workshop into the daily business that followed, promoting congruence with the Vision.

- Because the organisation had become accustomed to change, benchmark information was rapidly assimilated and processed by the team.

- The organisation was looking for direction and so quickly took ownership of the Vision without a major communication exercise.

- The Herrmann Brain Dominance Instrument indirectly revealed significant hidden talent in the team.

12

Aligning Internal Processes

We had made some serious headway. We had put some of the basic organisational building blocks in place at Sellotape Industrial. The new organisation structure had been designed to meet our objectives and we had cross-functional teams set up to close the gaps left by the inflexible nature of a traditional structure. We had also agreed on the culture and values we aspired to, and communicated the Vision to the organisation across the world. Managers from across the Company were using the teams that we had created to talk to one another and get to grips with opportunities as never before. But new obstacles that would hold us back from realising our Vision began to appear. There was much more work to be done before the business could rise to meet the new challenges that we had set ourselves.

Chapter 10 describes some of the many factors that influence team performance and we now had a number of these lined up with what we wanted to achieve. However, there were still some factors that were hampering the effectiveness of our team. Two particular areas that proved difficult were the management processes and the reward system. Saying this, I don't wish to suggest that everything was tackled textbook-style, with each area being ticked off in a methodical fashion. On the contrary, everything was done 'on the hoof', so to speak, in my normal pragmatic way. When we came across something that looked as if it was getting in the way of what we were trying to do, I took hold of it and did something about it. By default, this usually meant that the most important issues were tackled first, as they tended to be those that stood out from the landscape as we cleared more and more of the trees that were obscuring our view.

One of the earliest problems to appear was the matter of reward systems. In hindsight, this was hardly surprising, as money is generally the first thing to pop into our heads when we are asked to do something over and above the norm. And, fair enough, we had thrown out all the old rules about who did what; so it was natural that the (usually unspoken) "What's in this for me?" should start to rumble away in the background. Virtually everyone could claim to have taken on new responsibilities and, as we know, any good manager can always come up with some or other compelling justification as to why he should be paid more. It was a problem that had genuine potential to become a serious threat to the business. If we responded to the pressure, we would end up with a substantial increase in our manpower bill and the profitability would take a significant knock. I could, furthermore, well imagine the response of the shareholders and employees alike if we kicked off Sellotape Industrial by paying ourselves more. This would suggest that we were paying only lip service to the whole profitability issue.

It was a conundrum. How could I reward the people fairly for their efforts, and give them an interest in the success of the enterprise, while at the same time keeping costs down? Some people had indeed taken on significant extra responsibilities and a lot more work. They did deserve bigger salaries. However, if I accommodated these few, I would have to do something for all the others who had taken on different roles or I would risk being accused of unfairness. With my back against the wall, I resorted to the only path open to me – boldness. I simply issued a decree that there would be no adjustment to salaries for any reason whatsoever, anywhere in the business, until the next scheduled annual review nine months later.

When all else fails, what else is there but the autocratic approach? I justified myself to myself using the excuse that a good leader adapts his leadership style to the situation he finds confronting him, but I hoped desperately that this naked despotism would not destroy the collaborative and consultative culture that we needed to have operating throughout the business.

Fortunately, it worked. The staff accepted the freeze on salaries. I believe this was both because of their deep understanding of the problems associated with the issue and because they truly appreciated that we were trying to create a new and exciting business, which would end up being far more rewarding than just a few extra pound notes in the monthly pay packet. It was here that our investment in explaining the greater goals we were striving for to our staff paid off.

Having eliminated any possibility of more pay, the matter very quickly disappeared from everyone's personal agenda. After all, if there was no scope for winkling more money out of the Company, there was no point in thinking about it or talking about it, either to one's manager or one's mates. With the exciting prospects ahead of us, there were no significant defections, either.

In fact, the clear directive turned out to be much better for morale than an ongoing debate about salaries. Experience has taught me not only that this would have left more people dissatisfied than pleased, but also that people generally respond and adapt to well-defined boundaries and discipline in their work environment. Moreover, they tend to be all the happier for them. For those sceptics out there, I always refer to the navy when needing to justify this approach. Morale and team spirit is generally high on a ship and there is no more disciplined body of people than the crew of a warship.

This having been said, clearly people won't and shouldn't work forever on vague promises; so we needed to devise a financial reward system that was aligned with our goals, without an up-front hit to the profits. We started to look at a new kind of bonus scheme.

The history of bonus schemes at Sellotape had always been unfortunate, to say the least, with all manner of varieties having been tried out without much success. Previous attempts had varied from no bonus scheme at all, through arrangements dependent on local country profits, to so-called discretionary schemes, (in which discretion was used as a reason for not paying a bonus). On top of this medley, the hurdle levels for earning a bonus had often been far too ambitious. This simply left people disillusioned and cynical about the whole idea when they failed to earn anything following a year of hard work. The net result had been that, far from improving performance, the bonus arrangements had driven divisions into the business and led to disenchantment. A new and innovative approach was desperately needed. Ideally, we wanted a scheme that would reinforce all the kinds of behaviour and action we wanted, while at the same time providing a well-deserved reward for the added responsibility which almost everyone had taken on. If we got it right, at the end of the year, people would look back and see how their increased responsibilities and commitment had helped generate bigger profits, from which they were finally benefiting themselves.

So much for the theory. In fact, I soon discovered just how difficult it was to design a bonus scheme that was fair and motivating to everybody, that encouraged teamwork and that supported the overall prosperity of the business. After many drafts and long debate, we finally opted for three different schemes: one for the Senior Management Team, another for the country MDs who were not members of the Senior Team, and a third for everyone else in the business. There were, however, some basic principles that were common to all three schemes:

- They were based on a percentage of basic pay.

- The scheme would only pay for achieving the budget profits or better. (I did not want to reward under-performance in any way.)

- All the schemes had the same profit multiplier, which increased the bonus exponentially with the profit, once the budget threshold had been breached.

- The formulae were designed to encourage both collaborative work and local performance where appropriate.

- The profit used for determining the bonus had to be one which the individual felt able to influence.

In my previous career, I had often been the subject of bonus schemes that were so complex that it was virtually impossible for anyone to understand how they could influence what they would eventually get paid. I wanted to avoid this trap at Sellotape Industrial and sought to devise something simple that would act as a real incentive to everyone to improve performance. It all ended up somewhat more complicated than I had hoped. (Fig 12.1)

But, by setting it all out in straightforward terms and translating all the profit percentages into the currency of each country in which we were operating, we managed to get most of the organisation motivated to some degree by the prospect of a bonus. At the very least, what we developed did not reward behaviour that went counter to our overall goal.

For credibility's sake, it was also important that people believed

Senior Management Team

Bonus = (5% of Basic Pay) x (SI Profit Factor)

Country MDs

Bonus = (5% of Basic Pay x (0.5 x SI Profit Factor + 0.5 x Local Profit Factor)

All other employees

Bonus = (5% of Basic Pay) x (Local Profit Factor)

SI = Sellotape Industrial consolidated profit
Profit Factor determined from the table below

PFOFIT	Less than Budget	0 to 2% over Budget	2% to 5% over Budget	5% to 10% over Budget	10% to 20% over Budget	20% to 30% over Budget	More than 30% over Budget
FACTOR	Zero	1.0	1.5	2.0	3.0	4.0	5.0

Fig 12.1 - Sellotape Industrial bonus scheme

that there was a realistic chance that they might actually get some money out of the scheme. This meant that we needed to be working against a realistic budget. We had agreed that we wanted a culture of success. Fundamental to this was a budget that we could meet (or even beat) and that we could feel good about while going about the task. Fortunately, having learnt from bitter experience that using the budget as some sort of target to drive up performance simply did not work, the shareholders had already approved a budget that we all believed was achievable.

Another problem, which had dogged the organisation for some time, was the way in which we managed projects or, more precisely, mismanaged them. I had introduced projects as a way of making changes and improvements in the Operations function some years back and at about the same time, Jacques Tencé had started using a project approach to the work he was doing as a consultant in the Sales and Marketing areas.

Franck and Rory had responded in kind, quickly cottoning on to this project lark as a marvellous way of getting lots of activity going. So, they had joined in the fray by creating a stream of initiatives of their own. Projects had become fashionable and soon there was something of a competition to see who could create the longest list of initiatives. In no time at all, the whole business was awash with projects.

It all came to a head one day, while I was still doing the Group Operations job, when Franck parachuted into the Swiss plant. The normal routine was for Franck to meet with each of the project leaders and the local management to conduct a review of the projects. This time, it meant his having to review upwards of fifty projects, with objectives ranging from reducing the stationery costs at one end of the scale, to capital investment programmes worth hundreds of thousands of pounds at the other. For their part, the managers, often with four or five projects on the go at the same time, frequently became confused as to which project they were supposed to be reporting on, as well as the objectives they were supposed to be working to. There were also endless calculations of resource requirements and availability based on very dodgy assumptions, none of which anyone truly understood. The whole thing was something of a circus and the inevitable lack of progress drove Franck crazy. He would verbally lay into the poor, confused leaders in an attempt to get something to happen. At the time, I remember calling to mind a picture I had seen of a peasant thrashing an innocent donkey that was attempting to pull a heavy cart. The result in each case was zilch!

Of course, while all this was going on, nobody had the time or the energy to attend to their normal jobs and the performance of the business started to slide. A change was urgently needed.

There were a number of fundamental problems in the way projects were being handled:

- We were not clear on what was and what was not, a project. Anything that looked like a good idea got labelled 'a project'.

- There were just too many projects around. We did not have enough people or sufficient combined mental capacity to deal with them all.

- The individual roles necessary in a project, such as sponsor, initiator and leader, were not appreciated and therefore not defined.

- Anybody with managerial authority could initiate a project and simply dump it on an unsuspecting manager of lesser rank to execute.

● All projects were considered to be equally important. Reducing the amount of photocopying was treated in the same way as a major investment project that would benefit the whole business.

It was clear that if Sellotape Industrial was to succeed, I had to find a way to bring the project mania under control.

First, we agreed on what was to be called 'a project' (Fig 12.2). Then we described the individual roles within a project and what their responsibilities were to be (Fig 12.3).

What is a project? - Definition

A project:

● is an activity which will change performance (cost, quality or service or revenue)
● has a beginning and an end
● requires more than one person to make the change
● has a measurable input and output

'All step change improvements take place by project.'

Fig 12.2 - Project definition

All of this was reasonably simple, being no more than an adaptation of well known project management disciplines. Deciding how to manage and control the large number of projects, however, represented more of a challenge. Defining who could launch a project and putting 'gatekeepers' in place would control the number of new projects being created; but this would still leave us with the many current projects and no real mechanism for handling them. Some kind of infrastructure had to be put in place to manage the range of projects across the business.

We began by grouping the projects in terms of their importance to the business. By doing this we could allocate responsibility for

Project Roles

Initiator: The person who wants the project launched

Gatekeeper: Person or formal body responsible for
                   evaluating cost and benefit of the project, prior
                   to it being established. Has the authority to
                   turn down a project. Defines how benefits will
                   be measured (may not be financed). Closes
                   the project down.

Sponsor: An individual who legitimises the change and
                   who helps the project by removing obstacles.
                   May give advice but is not usually a member of
                   the project team.

Team Leader: Person who accepts leadership of the project.
                   Responsible for delivering the outcome. His
                   authority to requisition team members and
                   control their work.

Fig 12.3 - Project roles

managing projects to appropriate levels of management, who were, more than likely, the most capable of controlling the work. It was usually they who would benefit most from the success of the project and they who had the greatest interest in it. This also ensured that top management would not need to be involved in things like the number of photocopies we made, allowing them to concentrate on those projects that would make a real difference to the Company as a whole. We thus created a project management hierarchy. (Fig 12.4)

Within each category, we designed guidelines to help categorise projects, gave some ideas on who should fill each of the roles, and suggested an overall reporting regime. (Fig 12.5)

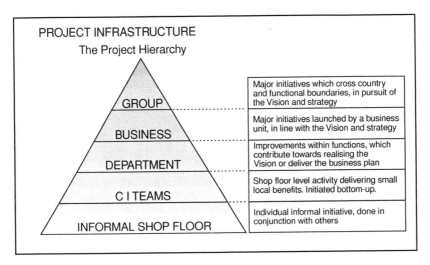

Fig 12.4 - The Project Hierarchy

The effect that this had can be compared to the reaction of drowning men being thrown a life belt – everyone grasped at the framework with delight and relief. It succeeded in bringing order to an area where previously only chaos had reigned. This structure also empowered more people to take responsibility for deciding what projects they should initiate in their own departments or businesses, rather than have the higher echelons deciding for them. At the top level, we were able to concentrate our attention on the two or three things that would make a real difference to the business. Gone were the myriad lesser initiatives which had plagued our lives, about which, if the truth were told, we often knew little of the real nitty-gritty. And we had, at last, found a way of controlling Franck's urge to create a multitude of projects every time he ran out of cigarettes and needed something to keep his hands busy.

Projects had also caused us problems within the R&D departments. There had been a tendency to take on too many initiatives without thought of the cost of the development work, the chances that anything saleable would be delivered, or the value of any forthcoming sales. Much to the frustration of Sales, with so many developments in the system at any one time, nothing positive ever seemed to come out the other end. And the more frustrated Sales got, the more new

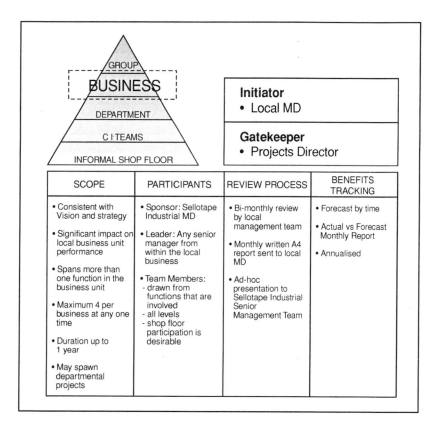

SCOPE	PARTICIPANTS	REVIEW PROCESS	BENEFITS TRACKING
• Consistent with Vision and strategy • Significant impact on local business unit performance • Spans more than one function in the business unit • Maximum 4 per business at any one time • Duration up to 1 year • May spawn departmental projects	• Sponsor: Sellotape Industrial MD • Leader: Any senior manager from within the local business • Team Members: - drawn from functions that are involved - all levels - shop floor participation is desirable	• Bi-monthly review by local management team • Monthly written A4 report sent to local MD • Ad-hoc presentation to Sellotape Industrial Senior Management Team	• Forecast by time • Actual vs Forecast Monthly Report • Annualised

Fig 12.5 - Example - Detail of Business Projections within the Project Hierarchy

product ideas they injected into the R&D department, in the vain hope that perhaps they might one day get something new that they could actually go out and sell.

If we were to devise new technologies and products to move us into areas of the market where we could earn better margins and so get our profits up, we were going to have to get a lot smarter at developing new products. We put together a team and charged them to find a new way of managing our R&D effort. The team designed a structured process in which all proposals for new products were carefully evaluated for their potential value before they got anywhere near the laboratory. Gatekeepers were appointed to keep control of the ideas or product requests that were actually allowed to go into R&D. They also ensured that what came out of development matched what had been requested in the first place. However, we found that we also needed to put an absolute limit on the number of projects that R&D could work on at any one time, to make sure that our meagre resources were focused on the few things that we thought would make the most money. By slashing the number of things that R&D were expected to work on, we at last started to get some commercially viable products that Sales could go out and sell. Besides earning us revenue, it also went to prove that Sellotape Industrial was indeed a technically capable Company.

By establishing Business Teams and the project hierarchy, and by empowering more people to make decisions across the Company, we had in fact delegated a lot of authority to others to make changes. As a result, many more of our managers suddenly found themselves needing capital investment ('Capex' as it was known) to make their own improvements.

Previously, only the most senior managers had ever been involved in justifying Capex, because it was considered to be a difficult and important process. Over time, through a combination of coaching and trial-and-error, the senior managers had become pretty good at pulling together a good case. As a privately owned company, we controlled capital expenditure very carefully, but sound justifications with well-defined returns were nearly always approved. By contrast, proposals with vague or unspecified returns inevitably got short shrift, and any attempts that claimed theoretical savings that would not be realised in hard cash were guaranteed to be thrown out.

What we now had was a new tranche of managers who lacked the benefit of this hard-won experience of developing and submitting capital investment proposals and, naturally enough, even their best efforts generally did not come up to scratch. This meant that I was constantly rejecting the vast majority of the requests that landed on my desk as being unfit to go to the Board.

The managers slowly but surely began to get frustrated at what they perceived as my obstinacy and tight-fistedness, while I, for my part, was getting sick and tired of spending my time reviewing poorly thought out and badly presented Capex requests. What really got up my nose were the 'panic requests' – those where the chaps who wanted the money had spent months messing around with building their case, only to dash into my office an hour before a Board meeting with a Capex proposal in their hands, expecting instant approval. It was a situation that could not go on indefinitely.

At the same time, I was starting to realise that, but for their poor drafting, some of the proposals that I was rejecting actually offered us considerable scope for improving our performance. We needed a better process for making decisions on capital expenditure, both in order to maintain the commitment and team spirit we had worked so hard to develop, and to bring my blood pressure under control.

I called a working group together. It was made up of all those managers who were new to the game of justifying capital investment, some of the old hands and myself. The managers arrived, each, as I had requested, with a list of what they thought was wrong with the way we managed Capex. A bun fight was in the offing and the managers had built up a good head of steam. They were not going to lose this opportunity to tell me what a crap job I was doing of this Capex thing.

This was just what I wanted – the old 'letting off steam' process I had used so many times before. They had to get all the frustration out of their systems before we could have a sensible debate. When the moment came, the lads let me have it: inconsistent rules, no feedback on why proposals had been rejected, lack of appreciation of the problems, hurdles too high, our disinclination to invest and a string of other complaints.

When the fan had stopped turning, it was my turn. I had also prepared a list of what was wrong with the Capex process. After all, I wanted an opportunity to let off steam as well. To bring matters to a head, I put up a slide, which said something like this:

I've heard your problems with Capex, now listen to mine ...

- Justifications in which the sums don't add up correctly.
- Justifications based on benefits that will never actually appear in the profit.
- A mentality of fixing problems by throwing money at them.
- Proposals in which the implications have not been thought through or understood.
- Projects arriving on my desk at the last moment, expecting instant approval.

The Result: I spend too much time examining, checking and redirecting Capex proposals to ensure that we are investing wisely.

Having bashed the ball back and forth until we were all exhausted, we agreed that it was time to call the game a draw and get on with developing a workable basis for the future.

In fact, no detailed or complex procedures were necessary. What we had been using had been sound and workable. All we needed was a common understanding of what we were trying to do as a business and how we wanted to go about it. What followed was a discussion about the philosophy and attitude to capital investment that we ought to have at Sellotape Industrial. Ours was not an investment-led strategy whereby we intended simply to buy new technology and machines to beat the competition. Instead, we had chosen to optimise what we had, investing in improvements wherever we could, while looking for creativity and flair in the way we tackled it all. Yes, our payback hurdles were high, but there were plenty of projects around that could give us the fast returns we were looking for; so there was little need to invest in projects with long payback periods. What was lacking, simply because we could not handle them all, was some kind of arbitration and vetting system for those proposals that met the payback criteria. We agreed that those projects which took us in the direction of the overall Vision would receive priority support.

We also worked through the implications of the return-on-capital-employed target we had in our Vision and reaffirmed how this target needed to kept firmly in view whenever the question of investment was raised.

This session proved to have been a very good use of management time. From that day on, Capex became something that we talked about in positive terms rather than being the butt of bitter recrimination. Managers began to discuss where to invest our money to get the best returns. Moreover, they grew to a level of maturity where project sponsors would voluntarily withdraw a project in favour of one put up by a colleague with a better return. I also encouraged managers to seek guidance from me in drawing up justifications. This meant that I had usually been involved in the preparation of major proposals before they appeared on my desk and so had little option but to approve them. Life became a lot less tense for us all and the business started to invest both rapidly and wisely for its future prosperity.

Management Stuff

The internal processes for making decisions and communicating them must be aligned with the vision and the objectives of the organisation, or the effectiveness of the Company will be adversely affected.

Managing projects:
Where an organisation generates a large number of projects, an infrastructure is needed to manage them collectively.

- The project infrastructure must manage the projects collectively.

- The projects themselves should be executed individually.

- All those involved in projects, (participants, leaders and sponsors) need to be trained in the basic principles of managing projects.

- Proposals for projects should be qualified through a structured process before resources are allocated to them. (Fig. 12.6)

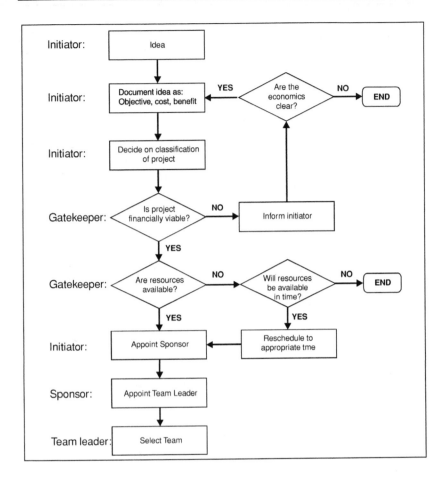

Fig 12.6 - Process for initiating a project

- A structured approach to R&D projects is required to ensure that the number of developments is limited and that resources are focused upon those developments that have the greatest potential return for the business.

Bonus scheme:

- The hurdle heights for earning a bonus must be set at a level at which there is a realistic possibility of them being cleared.

- To establish credibility, a bonus scheme should be designed so that most participants benefit from it in the first period of operation.

Capital Expenditure:

Managers who are charged with justifying capital expenditure need to be trained in:

- the accepted justification procedure
- the company philosophy and attitude to capital expenditure.
- The concept of return on capital employed.

13

The Franco-Prussian war

Merging Sellotape Industrial into a single global entity offered us the occasional opportunity to rationalise various elements of the original business that had previously operated independently. For example, we had a warehouse and conversion operation in France and a similar, but larger, operation not too far away in Germany. The economic case for rationalisation looked unarguable. We could close the French warehouse and transfer this activity to Germany, while maintaining the sales and order processing as they were in France. We felt sure that the customers would not know the difference. That was the theory, anyway.

After a lot of work planning the move, we duly closed the French warehouse and transferred all the goods to Germany. As one would expect when one makes a substantial change in a stable organisation, there were a few teething problems, which, being just teething problems, we felt sure would soon go away. The only problem was, instead of disappearing, they got worse as time went by. Product was delivered late; the wrong products were delivered; orders got lost; there were rejects due to poor quality. You name the problem, we had it! A thoroughgoing review revealed a whole bundle of technical issues had been overlooked when we had been preparing for the change. For one, the computer systems in France would not talk to those in Germany. Then, the slitting machines in Germany could not make some of the products they needed in France and the German warehouse was struggling to cope with the extra work. Oh, bugger! we said, feeling very embarrassed at having done such a shabby job of executing this project. We proceeded to roll up our sleeves to put things right. It was indeed a mess and it took some considerable time and effort to sort it all out. Eventually, however, everything was in place and we dusted off our hands and went away, confident that the nightmare was over.

Some hope! The customer complaints grew louder than ever, with some customers deciding that they had had enough and were going over to the competition. The business was beginning to suffer badly and we had to get to the bottom of the problem. I asked Jean Boisgontier, the French MD, what was going on. He immediately cited a long list of sins that the Germans had committed.

"It's all their fault," he complained, adding bitterly, "We never had problems like this when we had the warehouse in France." It was also evident that he felt that his opposite number in Germany was completely insensitive to the problems that they were experiencing in France. Indeed, from the French perspective, it looked as if the Germans hadn't the slightest interest in their problems. Having been persuaded that it was the German side that was to blame, I resolved to beat them about the head a bit. I phoned Harald Spönagel, the MD of Sellotape Germany.

"Listen Harald," I said somewhat brusquely, "We are losing sales in France, because you are giving them such lousy service. They are your customers as well, you know."

Harald had been in charge of the German operation for many years and he took considerable pride in running the business with Teutonic efficiency. He was in no mind to put up with any nonsense from me.

"I don't know why you're having a go at me," he said. "It is those French people who are the problem. Their forecasts are hopelessly wrong; they return perfectly good product as quality rejects and, no matter what we agree, they always want something different. Even when they send me the addresses to put on the labels, they then turn round and send the goods back, complaining that they cannot be delivered because the address is wrong," he protested. "It is unpossible to work like this!" (We had tried for months to persuade Harald that the word was 'impossible', with no success.)

I was familiar enough with the situation to know that everything Harald said was true. But, then again, so were the complaints coming from Jean in France. The only way forward would be to get everyone to agree on what the problems actually were. It was time to get the warring parties together, eyeball to eyeball, and hammer out the terms of a truce.

The four of us – the French and German MDs, myself as facilitator and Jacques Tencé (in his psychiatrist guise, to make sure nobody went berserk and committed murder) – convened at the French offices, which were attached to the now-empty warehouse near Basle. We began with each side listing all the problems as they saw them from their side of the border. Then, we worked through them all until we had a list of items that everyone agreed represented the real problems and that were not just the perception of one party. It was fascinating. All the anger and frustration was in fact being generated by a string of minor issues, each borne largely out of misunderstanding. Here we had the MDs of two substantial businesses having to get involved in solving such petty problems as where labels were placed on boxes and customer address details – problems that could have been solved by people at the very lowest level in the organisation. And here lay the basis for all the difficulties. For some reason or other, those at the coalface were not talking to one another.

"Is it a language problem?" I asked, going for the most likely cause of all this drama. "No," they assured me. Everyone involved could speak the language of the other side.

What was happening was this: when a problem arose at the French end, it would be sent all the way up the management hierarchy to the MD. He would then send a fax to his opposite number in Germany, together with a few emotive comments of his own just to make the point that he was not happy. Harald, by then very annoyed by the criticism from Jean, would send angry instructions down the chain of command in his organisation, telling his staff to sort out the problem immediately. Naturally, by the time the message actually got to the appropriate operator in the warehouse or the sales order processing clerk, the detail had been so twisted and distorted that it bore no relevance whatsoever to the actual problem they were having back in France. And, naturally, the same thing happened with messages going the other way.

Back at the truce talks, we eventually came up with an idea that might resolve the problems. We agreed that, if we could get all the problems tackled by the people on both sides of the border at the lowest level, the pieces would fall into place. If, we reckoned, we left the issues in the hands of those who initially faced the problem and kept management out of the way as much as possible, we would probably succeed in minimising the detrimental consequences of the Chinese whisper effect. It was certainly worth a try and it could only improve the situation. After all, who was more likely to know more about the issues involved – the management or the operators?

We resolved to break the log-jam using the subsidiarity principle – allowing problems to be solved at the lowest possible level in the organisation. Thus, each person in the French office would have a 'partner' in the German operation who did the equivalent job, whom they knew, understood and trusted. Then, if something went wrong, say in France, the person who had the problem could talk directly to his or her partner in Germany and between them they would find a solution that would satisfy everyone. It was clear that this approach would almost certainly solve most of the problems that were now plaguing the two businesses. Any more difficult issues could be allowed to drift up the management hierarchies, but only up to the lowest possible level at which they could be sorted out. Only major business issues should ever get to the ears of the two MDs. We felt really chuffed. We had a really neat solution on paper; but how, we asked one another, were we going to make it happen in real life?

The solution was there, staring us in the face. We had succeeded in resolving some seemingly intractable problems by having the two sides in one room discussing the issues in an atmosphere of mutual respect, with the overriding goal of finding an answer. The relationship between the MDs of France and Germany was now on a sound footing (a matter that had been helped along in no small way by our having shared an excellent French dinner together, washed down by some fine local wine). If this process worked for the MDs, then why not for their staff? We decided that we needed a Franco-German supply workshop, bringing together all those who were involved in the supply chain between the two Companies. The objective of this event would be twofold. Firstly, it would provide an opportunity and an environment in which strong personal relationships could develop between the various partners (whom we had identified). Then, based upon these relationships, we would get the partners to agree on how they would work together to satisfy the customers in their respective fields of activity. If all went according to plan, at the end of the workshop, we would have strong personal relationships in place connecting the French and German operations at a number of levels, and a set of rules that the various partners themselves were committed to and wanted to work by.

Unfortunately, I could not make the workshop, but I heard from reliable sources that, after an evening of good French food and drink, a new camaraderie was established which carried through into a productive working session. The two MDs led the activities, showing a united front and a determination to jointly put an end to all the internal bickering that had gone on for so many months. Having shared time, food and wine with one another, both the French and German contingents realised that their 'foreign' colleagues were not so bad after all and that everyone really did want to solve the problems. After a good day's interaction during which the working procedures were agreed and documented, everyone returned home feeling that they were at last in a position to restore their own working lives to normality. True, our phone bill showed a sharp leap in calls between France and Germany as these new-found friends kept their relationships alive and solved the daily problems; but it was a price we were glad to pay. Customer complaints in France immediately began to die away and very soon they all but disappeared.

Management Stuff:

In an inter-company supply relationship between two business units, communication needs to be structured to ensure that problems are resolved at the lowest possible level of the organisation.

- Multi-level links were established between the two businesses. (Fig 13.1)

- Individuals with comparable job functions and responsibilities were appointed at each level with the responsibility for and authority to resolve issues.

- A process was put in place to facilitate the development of personal relationships between corresponding individuals from the two businesses.

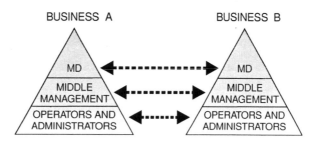

Fig 13.1 - Multi-level relationships between business units involved in inter-company supply

- Operating procedures were developed and agreed by those who were to be responsible for carrying them out.

- The process was led by the heads of the two business units, who themselves jointly developed the principles upon which the whole relationship was to be based.

14

A New Approach to the Market

Right from the time when I first joined Sellotape, I found the business inward looking, focused upon improving what it did and how it did it. The early stages of Sellotape Industrial were much the same. We formed teams in order to improve our communications and hence solve problems, which was very effective as a strategy: efficiency improved considerably; we became much more cost effective, and we delivered a more reliable service to our customers. We focused on developing our technologies and began to deliver a stream of new value-added products that would increase the premium we could demand in the market place. The air of panic that once pervaded the organisation was supplanted by one of calm professionalism and we began to grow confident that we could make this into an exciting business that others would want to emulate.

Soon the business indicators began to move in the right direction and the profit edged upwards. At last, we were looking like a quality operation. Only one problem remained; we seemed unable to grow our sales.

Sales had been more or less static for several years, but, given the problems we had had with our delivery, quality and response to customers, that was only to be expected. We all believed that, once we had sorted out our internal difficulties, sales would pick up automatically. After all, if sales had continued to hold up, despite the way we had abused our customers and ignored the market, then surely, once we were efficient, we would be able to sell more. And yet, despite the fact that we were no longer making it difficult for customers to do business with us, the growth was just not materialising.

We had revitalised the Sales functions across the business and brought in new blood to stimulate the demand. We had rebuilt the export department, after it had been all but disbanded some years previously, and we had the whole organisation focused on satisfying our customers. And yet, the sales remained stubbornly flat. My efforts at persuading and cajoling the Sales chaps had resulted in nothing positive either. Try as we might, nothing seemed to work. There could only be one explanation; there was something wrong with the way we were approaching the market. It was time to stop looking inwards and to turn our eyes to boundaries beyond those of our own organisation. We had to start thinking about the world outside and how we interacted with it.

Jacques and I called together a small working party to address the question of why we couldn't grow our sales. We wanted new and fresh ideas, so we selected the members of the group from a cross-section of the organisation: a salesman from Sweden, another from the UK, our Marketing Manager, a Sales Manager from the UK and a scientist from R&D. We deliberately left out the Sales Directors, because we wanted a new set of creative thoughts and not a reworking of the same old ideas that had failed us in the past. Naturally, this left one or two of these directors with their noses out of joint, since they considered the matter to be a strategic issue and thus part of their domain. But, once we had explained that our approach was completely in line with our cultural vision of seeking to use and develop the skills available, they settled into a state of uneasy acceptance.

It was Richard Symes who, over the years that we had worked together, had frequently reminded me that:

"Every organisation is perfectly designed to achieve the results that it gets."

And, reverting to this axiom, I reasoned that our organisation was perfectly designed to be incapable of growing its sales. In the absence of any better ideas, I decided to use this concept as the basis upon which to tackle the problem. By dissecting the design of the business as it was, we might be able to pinpoint what was preventing us from growing our sales.

We began by reviewing the all too few successes in which we had managed to achieve some growth. This quickly revealed that, in some instances, we had gained sales by growing our share of the market, while in others we had created a new market by developing a unique product to solve a customer's problem. We examined the nature of these two kinds of experience and found that the capabilities and structures we had needed to capture market share were very different from those that we had used to create new markets. (Fig 14.1)

Market Creation	Market Share Growth
New markets	Taking share from competitors
Bespoke products	General products
New product design	'Me-too' products
Locally led development	Company-wide development
Fast development essential	Speed not critical, or practical
One customer	Sold to a market
Reactive	Pro-active
High margin	Typically low margin
Sold by a specialist	Sold by general sales force
Low minimum order quantity	High minimum order quantity

Fig 14.1 - The characteristics of the two kinds of sales growth

With Sellotape Industrial we had a single organisation, which was attempting to grow the business both by capturing share and by creating new markets. This was an operational contradiction. For example, our traditional approach to selling was to have salesmen going around trying to convince customers they needed some of the products in our portfolio. While this was a reasonable way to grow market share, it was clearly hopeless in terms of creating new markets. Here, we needed creative technical solutions to problems that often involved the development of new products.

Indeed, when a customer came to us looking for a solution to a unique problem, most of the organisation was at a loss in terms of knowing just how to deal with the enquiry. If such a product didn't appear in the price list then we were well and truly stymied. What tended to happen was that the customer got passed from person to person until he usually gave up and put the phone down.

Our structures and decision-making processes could not cope with a new opportunity of this kind. For a start, we did not trust the salesmen to make decisions on pricing products, let alone on technical design. Indeed, we laboured under the impression that salesmen would give the product away if we allowed them to. On the odd occasion that we did manage to capture an enquiry, by the time we came up with a product, the customer had often forgotten about ever having discussed the matter with us. The process of designing, creating and delivering a solution to the customer's problem usually became so wrapped up in bureaucracy that it sometimes took months to get a result. That we ever managed to create a sales demand by solving an occasional problem for a customer was only down to luck and the tenacity of a few technically capable sales people.

However, the fact that we were simply not good at taking advantage of market creation opportunities might just have been acceptable if we had been good at growing market share. But, the truth was that we were lousy at that, too. We seemed incapable of marketing our products or ourselves in any structured way. Furthermore, we were never quite sure if we had any competitive advantage in the marketplace and if we had, what it actually was. It certainly wasn't cost. In our attempts to be flexible, we had sacrificed some economies of scale and therefore were a comparatively high cost operation. Nor were we selling unique products; so we could hardly claim any advantage over the competition there. To add to this, since we did not study the markets to identify what products were needed, choosing instead to develop products based on requests from individual customers, we tended to concentrate on variations on existing products. Structurally speaking, we were probably better designed to capture share than to create new markets, but only marginally so. We were not streamlined for either purpose.

This was really worrying. We had carefully developed structures and created tasks, decision-making processes, teams and information systems. It had all been designed to make us into a slick and smart business and, as far as it went, all this had worked very well for us in terms of improving our overall efficiency. However, it now appeared as if everything we had done was in fact standing in the way of our growth. The realisation that we might have been so wrong, after all the work that we had done over that past year or so, shook me rigid. Surely, I told myself, it couldn't be true. But, slowly, we were forced to accept that, although we had created a structure that was ideal for improving the business efficiency, from the market perspective, we had a one-size-fits-all organisational design and culture that just didn't match up to the requirements for either share growth or market creation. Sellotape Industrial was neither fish nor fowl, but some horrible hybrid. Richard had been right. We were indeed perfectly designed for the rather poor results we were achieving.

Our first desire was to be able to grow our sales by creating new markets, because this was the most profitable route. When one solves a problem for a customer, the very last thing to be discussed is the price. This opens up the possibility for good margins. However, since most of our business was based on products that had other equivalents in the market, we could not ignore the need to grow our market share. If we did not do this, not only would our growth be desperately slow, but we also ran the risk of being buried by the competition. We had to be able to do both – to grow our market share and to create new market opportunities. Like it or not, this meant that we needed two very different kinds of organisation.

At this point I confess to having lost the plot. My structured thinking style could not cope with the idea that a single business needed two completely different approaches to the market. We had a range of products and we had set up an organisation to sell these to our market. Surely, we could not have two kinds of organisational culture within a single business at the same time. OK, so we had to sell the same products to grow market share and also to create new markets. Well, that still sounded like just one organisation to me. Fortunately, Jacques came to my rescue. He was one of those 'yellow cap' people with a strong bias toward a creative thinking style. To him it was obvious.

"We have three kinds of business within Sellotape Industrial", he explained. "One is a 'Speciality' business, where we make our technical capability available to the customer. Another is the 'Core' business, where we provide products and solutions to match customer adhesive and sealing application needs. Then there is the third – the

'Basic' business – where we simply sell existing products to existing customers." This may have been obvious to Jacques, but to me it was gobbledegook.

"You are now talking about businesses – don't you mean markets?" I asked.

"No", said Jacques, "these are all businesses, because there is a whole infrastructure involved which includes everything from product development and production through to sales and the market." This was way outside my paradigm.

"Humour me, Jacques," I said. "Explain this to me as if I was your ten-year-old nephew." Jacques cast his eyes briefly to the ceiling and then sketched a table on the board. (Fig 14.2)

BASIC	Selling products to existing customers	Commodity products with low value-added content
CORE	Bringing solutions to customers' bonding and sealing applications needs	Standard product, with or without downstream customisation
SPECIALITY	Making our capability in adhesive and sealing technology available to solve the customer's problems	Unique formulations or presentations designed with and for the customer

Fig 14.2 - The three business areas in Sellotape Industrial

I was beginning to get a handle on the concept, but still needed to work on it some more. "So, are you saying, we need three different kinds of organisation to manage these three kinds of business?" I asked.

"No," came a quick reply. "The 'Basic' and 'Core' sectors need the same kind of infrastructure to support them. In both of these, we are selling more or less the same products to all our of customers as our competitors, and so we can manage these sectors in the same way." Jacques was enjoying exercising his creative nature and his talent for marketing.

"The 'Speciality' business is very different though. Here, we need to work with individual customers and not with the market as a whole.

165

The ways of capturing the opportunities and managing the process of meeting the customer's need have to be specifically designed to be fast, as well as technically and commercially smart." Well, that was a relief. At least I did not have to think about having three organisations within one!

Over the next few weeks, Jacques and I talked at length about this new view of the business and what it meant to us in reality. The two of us had to be absolutely clear in our own minds as to what the implications were and how we were going to adapt our organisation to this latest challenge. As we worked at it, I became more comfortable with what I still saw as a revolutionary development. We began to define the nature of the organisation needed to support the three business sectors. (Fig 14.3)

To apply these principles, we would need to redirect our efforts and resources. Putting a lot of work behind the 'Basic' business did not make too much sense, since the margins in this sector were low and the future of our business lay elsewhere. All this now seemed quite obvious when we looked at it from our new-found perspective. Unfortunately, we hadn't been looking at things that way before. Over the previous year we had spent masses of effort and money trying to sell commodity products – a strategy which had kept us busy, but had earned us peanuts. With what we now knew, we were certainly not going to repeat the same mistake.

When we thought about the 'Core' business, it was obvious that we needed to be able to manage our products far better, first in order to understand our market, and then to be able to focus our energies on exploiting the opportunities in the most profitable way. There was enormous scope for us to restructure the product range to correspond to the market needs much more closely. This would also allow us to vastly reduce the number of products that we sold; but, to tackle this properly, we would have to appoint product managers, since we didn't have any. We would also have to develop our capability for process development, so that we could continuously improve the way we manufactured these products and so drive the costs down. Purchasing would be another critical area, both so that we could reduce our purchasing costs and so that we could ensure that we contracted out the most suitable products in a way that would save us the most money.

BASIC	Make or buy decisions Supply management
CORE	Product management Structured cost reduction Focus on selling products in the portfolio Rapid response tailoring at the conversion stage Development of new products structured and controlled Low risk strategy (due to high cost of failure) Organisation disciplined in following procedure
SPECIALITY	Product development the primary focus Limited formality and control Fast reaction with little bureaucracy Commercial acumen instead of management control Technical selling Risk taking strategy (low failure cost) Organisation trained to be receptive to opportunities

*Fig 14.3 - The nature of the organisation and work needed
to support the three business sectors.*

It was, however, in the 'Speciality' area that we needed to really improve our act. Here – in the high margin niche areas – was where we saw the future of the business. This, we felt, would also become the engine room that would drive our technical development. The new technologies developed to solve a customer's problem today would be the basis of new 'Core' products that we would sell to the global market tomorrow. We would need a dedicated sales organisation for Specialities, staffed by talented and technically trained salespeople who were stimulated by the process of finding opportunities and developing products to exploit new markets. These salespeople would be the 'hunters' of the organisation, whereas the 'Core' and 'Basic' salespeople would be the 'farmers' with a largely stable client base that they serviced on a regular basis. We would also need a way of fast-tracking product development for 'Speciality' business, without losing control of what went on in R&D in terms of the overall needs of the business. Furthermore, we would have to keep our technical capability up to date and be completely familiar with the technology of the key customers with whom we would be working to develop unique products. This would mean a significant change in our attitude to our customer base. We would need to move away from the usual, somewhat adversarial supplier-customer relationship, towards one of building partnerships with our 'Speciality' customers – relationships in which we trusted one another and worked together as true partners for our mutual benefit.

Once I had fully grasped this radical new approach, I became very excited. I could see how it could unlock even more of the potential that was present in our people. By aligning all the functions and activities – from R&D through production, sales order processing, to sales and marketing – and matching the natural skills and attributes of our people, with the needs of the market, we should be able to leap forward to the next level of performance. My imagination was also seized by the thought of the gains in speed and all the other advantages that might accrue from close partnerships with key customers, when we pooled our R&D capabilities and knowledge. Besides inevitably driving up our sales and profitability, it would turn our key customers into allies with whom we would be able to work for the prosperity of us all.

The impact on Sellotape Industrial would potentially be huge, both in terms of the internal changes that were implicit and the possibilities that would open up to us in the marketplace.

It was time to redesign the company once again. And you can just imagine the initial reaction of the Senior Management Team when we told them. "Oh no, not again! We have only just recovered from the last upheaval." But it was only a short-lived reflex action. The team understood that, to be successful and grow, we had to keep adapting ourselves to the ever-changing environment in which we found ourselves, even if in this case it wasn't so much our environment that had changed, but us. We had created an organisation designed to optimise its internal capability and we had really succeeded. Now, we had a new purpose in mind and we had to metamorphose into a form that was designed to carry it out.

This time, however, we could not go for another 'Big-Bang' reorganisation. Firstly, it would take time for everyone in the

Company to fully grasp the radical new approach. After all, it had been something of a struggle for me to get to grips with it, so it would probably be just as much of a challenge for the rest of our staff. Second, we did not have the right mix of experience and skills. Although our people were well qualified and very capable of meeting the needs of the organisation at that time, were going to need different skill sets in the new organisation we were planning to create; skills that we had not previously sought to develop. We decided to go for evolution rather than revolution, resolving to convert to the new organisation over a period of about six months. This would allow the organisation to work through the process of understanding our new approach and give us time to develop people into the new roles that would be created along the way.

The long-term vision was for the Business Teams to evolve into stand-alone business units, which, individually and collectively, would take on the responsibility for the profitability of the business and everything that went with this. These business units would be made up of multi-cultural, cross-functional teams, in which the capabilities and skills were finely honed and completely aligned with market needs. Instead of each Business Team being designed around a product range and differing only slightly from one another, the new Business Units would be unique and designed specifically to meet the needs of the market segment they served, with management processes adapted accordingly.

Over the next few months, we progressively introduced the new organisational design. We made structural changes and appointed people to new posts, as they became capable of taking on the new responsibilities. We developed strong, close relationships with key customers and began working very closely with them on creating the technologies of the future. Along the way, we were increasingly reassured that we were indeed on the right track by the approval we got when we explained our new approach to the outside world – our customers, suppliers and other businesses.

In the UK, there was an interesting spin-off from this. As part of an exercise in planning the growth of our 'Speciality' business, we ran through how we might reel in new opportunities. We discussed the possibility that, through our reputation and marketing activity, someone with a problem might have heard that Sellotape Industrial was a company that solved adhesive problems, and would phone us to ask for help. Would we be agile enough to capture the enquiry and convert it into a sale? We decided to find out. We invented some problems that we knew we could resolve and then asked a few people to phone in, pretending to be potential customers. Well, we got a result; but hardly one that pleased us. Only two out of the five enquiries were captured! We obviously had a huge gap in our ability to see a potential opportunity and take advantage of it. Within a few weeks, we had designed a telephone skills training course and had rolled it out to everyone who used the phone.

Slowly, we began to build up a list of successes in the market and we started to develop a library of stories that we could use to explain what we did to the wider world. Among the successes was the flange sealing system we developed for a manufacturer of sectional tanks. This comprised a strip of foam contained in a U-section of butyl sealant that allowed for movement of the sections against one another. This neat product had the added bonus that the foam cleaned the butyl from the thread of the bolts used to fix the sections together. While this may not seem terribly exciting to most of us, to the tank manufacturer it was a revolutionary development that allowed him to build better tanks than his competition. Those readers who drive a well-known make of German luxury car will, in part, be enjoying a silent ride because there is a pad of our foam behind the number plate that prevents it from rattling. One of our products was even used in 'Thrust', the first land vehicle to travel faster than sound.

We were now well and truly on our way to becoming a world leader in our industry and we were also being taken seriously for our innovative management ideas.

Much to my regret, we never got to the end of the evolutionary process whereby the Business Teams were to become Business Units with full profit responsibility. In June 1997, before we got to the stage of making this transition, we were sold to the Scapa Group, whose priority was to integrate Sellotape Industrial into their operation. Our programme came to an end.

Management Stuff

Sellotape Industrial had been designed to address internal issues, without reference to the market or to any growth strategy. Once the internal problems had been resolved, the structure needed to be altered to enable the business to address the market more effectively.

To gain market share, the business had to focus on being better than the competition. This involved:

- cost reduction
- customisation at the end of the process
- structured new product development for the global market
- organisational discipline
- risk management.

To create new markets, the business needed a different set of capabilities, including:

- rapid product development
- delegated authority for commercial decisions
- minimum control and bureaucracy
- risk taking.

Within the business, there were three segments:

> **Basic** – selling products
> **Core** – selling solutions
> **Speciality** – selling capability

Each of these required different core competencies

- Basic:
- Outsourcing • Cost optimisation

- Core:
  - Product Management • Application selling

- Speciality:
  - Marketing • Customer relationship management
  - Rapid technical solution development

To develop these core competencies fully, the business needed to be divided into Business Units based upon the business sectors.

171

15

So What Did All This Achieve?

Sellotape Industrial came into being in July 1996 and we continued to run it as an entity until it was absorbed into the Scapa organisation in 1998. During this relatively short life span, we succeeded in creating a global business out of a disparate group of independent businesses. We introduced a completely new culture, new ways of working and reinvented ourselves twice over, radically transforming ourselves internally and fundamentally changing our whole approach to the market. We completely transformed the organisation and, in so doing, achieved something that had been thought impossible.

The words from a brochure that we published in July 1997 describe the kind of business we had created far better than I can.

"At Sellotape Industrial we have a shared vision of the future with the following four principles at heart:

Teamwork:

- In the workplace – solving problems and developing new processes

- With customers – finding the best solutions to their requirements

- With suppliers – looking for best materials and controlling costs

- In management – determining the best way forward

Empowerment:

- Giving authority where it counts – at the sharp end. Getting decisions made quickly by people who know. Using multi-functional teams to tackle difficult issues quickly and make their own decisions. Allowing everybody to add his or her unique contribution. Sharing the responsibility for the future prosperity of the business.

Investment in People:

- Continuously developing and growing individuals to accept greater authority for managing the business. We believe that this approach benefits both the individual and the company.

Performance:

- Taking pride in achieving the best results for the company, its customers and shareholders."

But was it worth all the anguish and hard work? What about these 'best results'- from the shareholders point of view?

Sellotape Industrial was established half way through the financial year, when the profitability for the first six months was about 5% of sales. Rory challenged me to raise our game to a level that would return 6.5% of sales for the full year. In the event, we turned in 7.4%. During those first six months of the transformation, we also managed to shake out a lot of cash, a large portion of which came from reducing the inventory by almost £1 million. (Fig. 15.1)

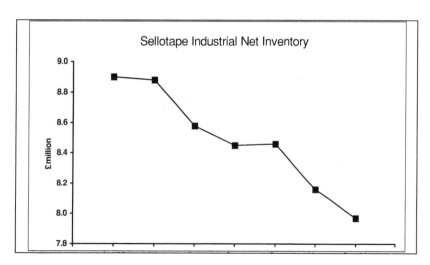

Fig 15.1 - Inventory June to December 1996

This represents just one snapshot illustrating the speed with which the new organisation made a real difference to the performance of the business in the early stages.

Beating this target marked a real high for both managers and workers, because, for most of us, it was the first time in many years that we had been part of a team that had actually exceeded the performance goals. It felt good to be successful and this early win bred further success later on.

This trend of improved performance continued right up to the point at which Sellotape was absorbed into Scapa Tapes. This does not mean to say that it was a smooth ride all the time. Far from it. There were many bad months along the way that added to my, by then, growing crop of grey hairs. But, when we looked back over each quarter and each half-year, we could see that these were just bumps in the road that we were travelling along in our pursuit of higher and higher levels of performance.

In the end, it was our Swiss operation – our largest manufacturing plant – which made the biggest contribution to the changes in the company fortunes. The plant had been losing money for several years before it was incorporated into Sellotape Industrial, with each of the initiatives that had been launched in an attempt to turn the business around ending in failure. Even Franck had had a go a being the MD. But that had only made things worse. Franck was a good CEO, but he made a lousy job of being the MD of an operating business. He openly admits that he is good at 'making mess' in an organisation and then leaving it to others to clear up after him – hardly the ideal profile for an operational MD.

In a state verging on desperation, we asked Dieter Pfaff if he would take on the job of MD. Dieter had been the Purchasing Director of the Swiss operation for many years and, while he was the consummate buyer, he had no experience of running a business. Nevertheless, he accepted the challenge of turning this monster around. Shortly after he was appointed, I attended one the first general meetings Dieter held with his management and staff. I have a vivid memory of him explaining passionately to the gathering that his only goal in life was to turn in just one Swiss Franc profit from the business over the next year. In fact, it took him only a few months to realise this goal. By providing the leadership for which the people had been yearning for years, Dieter instilled a new spirit in the organisation, mobilising every individual to seek creative ways of improving the performance of the business. Despite previous rounds of cost reduction, the people themselves found many more opportunities to reduce overheads by substantial amounts, developing new and creative way of running the business more effectively. The profitability of every product was systematically analysed, and those that were not paying their way were dealt with by reducing the cost, by technical development or by repositioning in the market. Within a year, his business had become the largest profit generator in the whole of Sellotape Industrial and the benchmark against which we measured the performance of all our other operations.

It was Dieter's drive and leadership that made Switzerland into a success story, while it was the culture and organisation that we created which gave him support and provided opportunities for him to exercise his talents, doing what he knew needed to be done.

By focusing on developing the 'Speciality' business and careful managing the gross margin in every part of the business, we succeeded in raising our gross margin to over thirty percent – somewhat more interesting than the low twenties we had been accustomed to. This, combined with tight control and an imaginative reduction of fixed costs, delivered a steady improvement in profitability over the life of the business, breaking through the 10% barrier for the 1998 financial year. (Fig. 15.2)

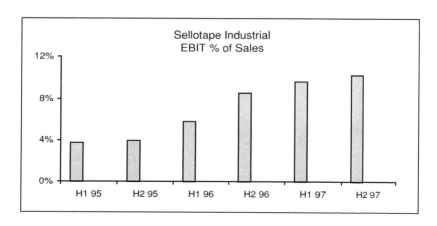

Fig 15.2 - Earnings before interest and tax as a percentage of sales

Our return on capital employed rose from the 9% we began with in 1995 to 15.6% for 1998, well beyond what we had hoped to achieve in such a short time. What is more important is that we did this without resorting to starving the business of investment to hold the capital base down. On the contrary, we continued our programme of judicious investment throughout and at no stage did any potential purchaser find evidence that we had under-invested in the business, or dressed it up for sale. In fact, our infrastructure turned out to be better than that of virtually every business that sought to acquire us.

Unfortunately, we were not able to complete the journey we had embarked upon, owing to the acquisition and the consequent change in priorities. This was a real disappointment for Jacques and myself, because we were denied the opportunity of realising our ultimate dream – of creating one of the best tapes companies in the world. But there is no point in wishful thinking. We both soon got over it because we had known all along that at some point we would be sold and that our dream was likely to be de-railed along the way. For our employees, being thrust into the arms of a new and largely unknown owner was threatening, because neither they nor we had any idea what their plans for Sellotape Industrial were. However, as it happened, the acquisition worked to the benefit of the vast majority of our workforce. We had a group of highly capable managers and workers who were skilled at their jobs and well versed in dealing with and managing change. Suddenly, we were part of a much larger business with more career development possibilities. To the delight of our new owners, the Sellotape Industrial people quickly found opportunities to display their talents and skills, and many were soon rewarded with even more interesting work and promotion.

So, in the final analysis, was it worth all the anguish and hard work? It most certainly was. What we did at Sellotape Industrial worked to the benefit of all involved. The shareholders realised a return on their investment in our vision; the management gained a set of valuable skills and experiences; the employees had their working lives enriched; and the new owners inherited what we had created.

Management Stuff

There is only one lesson: by sticking with the programme, we delivered the desired results in terms of the organisation, the culture and the financial performance.

16

A Backward Glance

This book has been all about the successes we achieved in the various change programmes we undertook at Sellotape. It says little about the mistakes, failures and difficulties we experienced along the way. I suppose it is human nature to remember what was good and to forget the bad. This ability to quickly forget all the unfortunate things one experiences is probably a prerequisite for being a change leader, because if one were to remember all the hardships endured in the process, it would be enough to put anybody off ever embarking on another change programme.

There are, however, probably as many lessons to be learnt from the failures as from successes. So, having trawled my subconscious to find a just few of the more spectacular mistakes we made, I feel duty bound to detail some of these, as well as some of my musings on the downsides and negatives that go along with the sort of change programme that we mounted. Anyone contemplating leading a culture change should be aware of these and extract whatever might be useful to them.

When I think back to the original Operations Vision programme, our first mistake was that we failed to take Sales along with us. This happened because we had huge internal problems within Operations and this had made us into the bad boys of the business, because we were incapable of satisfying the customers. We felt, at the time, that part of the problem lay in the degree of freedom that Sales had to push us Ops guys around. In consequence, we decided that we had to stand up for ourselves a little and not be walked over. Naturally, this caused some bitterness amongst Sales, but this was only to be expected. The main problem came about because we made no attempt to deal with this resentment. On the contrary, I certainly took some kind of perverse delight in metaphorically shoving my finger up their noses, which of course hardly helped improve relationships. Then, as our change programme gained momentum and the Ops people started to use the new management techniques, and the continuous improvement teams began to deliver results, a further divide developed between the cultures in Ops and Sales. We even detected a degree of envy amongst some of the more junior sales staff. "Why don't we have a Vision programme in Sales?" they began to ask.

This represented an opportunity missed and it was compounded on that fateful day when we, in the Ops team, sat around discussing how we should deal with the growing division between ourselves and Sales. With the animosity and distrust having its origins in the past, long before we launched the Vision programme, and with no simple way of closing the gap between us, we asked ourselves whether we should take the initiative and try to establish some common ground with the Sales guys. I have no doubt that we could have designed a process to close the chasm if we had chosen to. We had proved ourselves capable of solving far more difficult problems than this particular one. But, had we chosen to do so, it would have taken time and effort that would have diverted our attention away from what we were trying to get done in our own area. Having considered the options, we took a very conscious decision – to ignore the relationship issues with Sales and charge ahead with our programme regardless. We managed to persuade ourselves that Sales would simply be dragged along in our wake, and that it would all come together somehow later on.

Of course, this was a cardinal error. Doing this simply drove us further apart. Furthermore, the recognition we were getting for our programme from top management became something of an irritant and an embarrassment to the management in Sales, who began to throw rocks at our programme in a conscious or unconscious effort to discredit what we were doing. They campaigned on the platform that it was too costly, inappropriate for the business, too complicated, and out of touch with the real problems of the day. Our response in Ops was to build up our defences against these assaults and we began to create what became known as 'Fortress Ops'. We developed a mind-set of immunity to attack, leaving us free to continue with our programme, despite being under siege within the very business that we were trying to improve. The two sides continued to war with one another right up to the time when Sellotape Industrial was created. And, since it acted as a significant drag on our progress over the next year or two, the fall out from the past proved to be a source of considerable anguish to both my team and myself.

If I were able to go back and change any one thing that I did in the Ops Vision programme, it would be that fateful decision to charge ahead and leave Sales behind. If we had applied some of our efforts to at least maintaining diplomatic relations with Sales at that early stage, we would have avoided all the work and time we had to put into defending what we were doing later on. We might even have been able to mount a joint change programme with Sales as partners. This would have dramatically speeded up the improvement in the performance of the business.

There were also some minor mistakes I made that had a disproportionate impact on the programme. One example that sticks in my mind is an episode surrounding radios in the Dunstable factory. The factory operators had traditionally brought the odd portable radio from home to provide background music while they worked. While I had no problem with the music, I came under assault from our friendly neighbourhood Safety Officer because the electrical leads to these radios did not meet the required standards, making them a potential fire hazard. Any electrical device had to be permanently wired in place, I was sternly advised. After ignoring the matter for months, I began to receive formal letters from the Safety Officer making it clear that he expected some action. Since the radios didn't belong to us, we couldn't permanently wire them up and, with the cost of installing piped music being prohibitive, I could see no easy way of making him go away. I decided to use safety as the excuse to do what seemed to be the only option available to me – to ban personal radios from the plant.

The backlash was immediate, intense and sustained. I was accosted in the factory and asked to explain myself. Expressions of rage appeared the 'Letters to the Editor' column in the company magazine and the subject found its way onto the agenda of management meetings. Ignoring the outcry in the hope that it would die down only made matters worse. Eventually, I realised that what I had done was contrary to spirit of our Vision. I came to my senses and did what I should have done in the first place. I asked the operators to set up a team to come up with a solution that would keep the Safety Officer quiet and provide music for the operators, while not costing the company a fortune. Of course, the team came up with a simple solution that satisfied everybody in record time.

Change programmes are somewhat like medicine. They usually do you good, but they all have side effects. Very occasionally the side effects are worse than the disease that you hoped to cure in the first place. In our change programmes, there were no labels on the box to warn us of the side effects and so, when they occurred, they came as something of a surprise. Fortunately, the patient survived the treatment.

Change Programme medicine takes time to have an effect: time is always a major issue for any change programme. It takes time to shift the attitudes and values of an organisation and, while the use of skilful change management techniques can minimise the time taken, there is never a 'quick fix' solution.

In the early days, despite our having expended a lot of energy and time on the programme, there were few results to be seen and we came under intense pressure to write off the whole exercise as a failure. Some of my colleagues began to suggest that we should rather move onto some new initiative that might deliver a 'quick fix'. At that stage the support of my ever-stable and determined sponsor came to our rescue. Once again, it had been worth investing time up front to be certain that our sponsor knew that a change programme is a marathon, rather than a sprint.

Another aspect of the time problem is the amount that is absorbed in leading and executing the programme, as opposed to 'normal' work. We frequently had to deal with managers complaining that they could not cope with all the extra work in addition to their routine duties. The best response, we found, was to challenge them to reach deeper into their own capabilities and find ways of doing everything we asked. Almost without exception, people surprised themselves and us, by what they managed to achieve when they put their minds to it. And they grew as individuals in the process.

Creating a Vision for the future and getting everyone to take ownership of it was the core to most of what we did. But this approach can have its negative aspects.

Firstly, if one is successful in inspiring everyone in the organisation to take this dream into their hearts, then action generally breaks out spontaneously all over the place. Controlling this activity can become a problem. One needs to decide in advance how to focus this newly released energy and be ready to put the strategy in place immediately after communicating the Vision.

Another danger is that the very nature of a visionary change programme creates expectations amongst the workforce. This is, after all, the whole idea of enthusing everyone with the Vision. The risk is that individuals or groups may develop expectations in their own minds which are outside the scope intended by the change agent and sponsors. When it becomes apparent that these expectations are not going to be met, disillusion sets in and disaffection can spread, resulting in a general loss of commitment to the Vision. I think we managed to avoid this by spending so much time and energy making sure that everyone shared a common understanding of what the words in the Vision meant in real life.

People will also use the Vision as a stick with which to beat management. Whenever management does something unpopular or has to take a hard decision for good business reasons, the words of the Vision will be twisted or interpreted narrowly so as to suggest that what is happening is making a mockery of the Vision. We found that, as long as we were being true to the vision in its entirety, we could effectively rebuff such attacks without damaging the overall level of commitment to the Vision.

It is now obvious to me that we thrashed around somewhat blindly. It was almost by accident that we put our finger on most of the multiple components of a successful culture change programme. We might have been more effective if there had been a master plan to move all the various aspects of the programme forward together. With the benefit of hindsight, I subsequently drew up a schematic representation of such a master plan by cobbling together a number of elements from various programmes. (Appendix G)

Probably the most important thing we learnt from our experiences was that when you make a mistake, the best thing to do is to acknowledge quickly that you have got it wrong and then go and try something else.

Management Stuff

Key learning points

- Culture change programmes take time to deliver benefits.

- The sponsors of a culture change programme must be committed to the programme for the long term.

- The key stakeholders in any programme must be identified in advance and appropriate action taken to gain and maintain their support, lest they become saboteurs.

- Employees will evaluate every management decision against the espoused Vision and values. Any contradiction will lead to a delay in, or even prevent, the desired changes being realised.

- Employees must have a thorough understanding of the bounds of the Vision to ensure the expectations of individuals match those contemplated in the Vision.

- All the aspects of the change programme should be planned in advance so that the programme moves forward consistently on all fronts.

Co-author's Note

Since this book was completed, a number of the UK's manufacturing sectors have found themselves in considerable difficulty. Automotive, textiles and other industries are finding themselves faced by dramatic new challenges. On the other hand, as the experience at Sellotape shows, even apparently insuperable problems can be tackled and can lead to tremendous achievements.

The main questions that senior managers must ask themselves are:

- Is my business rock-solid and growing?

- If not, do I have the skills to lead a successful change programme?

- If not, what am I going to do about it?

Experience shows that, if a workforce is given a positive enough lead towards a sufficiently desirable vision, then they will usually follow and exceed all performance expectations.

With the challenges of the 21st century ahead of us, we must all confront the issue of managing change. Few laurels will be won by those who just sit there and cogitate. The spoils will go to those who just do it.

Stephen Lytton

Further Information

Robert Sullivan would be pleased to enter into discussions with companies undertaking or considering embarking on a change management initiative.

If you would like to discuss the matter further, please contact Steve Lytton on the following numbers:

Telephone: +44 (0) 1933 681009
Fax: +44 (0) 1933 682552
Mobile: 07970 075233
Email: s.lytton@clasp.org.uk

APPENDIX A

The Operations Vision   'A Professional Operation'

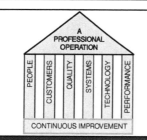

PEOPLE

- Effective teamwork, with good communications, mutual commitment and the freedom to act
- Pride and enjoyment in all that we do
- A safe, secure and pleasant working environment
- Mutual respect and trust in one another
- People development for the mutual benefit of the company and the individual
- Managers leading thinking people
- Self-managed teams
- A Company people want to work for

CUSTOMERS

- Excellent quality and service, as perceived by the customer
- Matched promise and capability
- Effective partnership from suppliers through to the customers
- Actively seeking customer feedback
- Meeting the needs of internal customers

PERFORMANCE

- Demanding the highest performance of people, materials and plant
- Linked performance measures relevant to every level of the organisation
- Recognition of individual and team performance
- Focus on areas of highest benefit
- Common goals driving co-ordinated activity
  - producer of high-value, low-cost goods
  - high stock rotation and flexibility
  - fast new product development

QUALITY

- A shared passion for quality in everything we do
- Exceeding expectations
- Ownership throughout the organisation
- Preventing things going wrong
- 'Right First Time' approach to repetitive activity
- Reducing overall cost of quality

SYSTEMS

- Relevant, accurate and on-line information at the point of action
- Documented procedures available in a simple format
- Compliance to highest international quality standards
- Close loop processes, completely linked with other areas
- Fast and effective transfer of knowledge

TECHNOLOGY

- An innovative approach to product design and processes and customer needs
- Low cost. Low waste, flexible manufacturing plant and processes
- Maximised output and capacity utilisation through reliable and consistent production equipment
- Building and services that promote efficient plant layout and high standards of housekeeping

CONTINUOUS IMPROVEMENT

- Everybody has two prime responsibilities:
  - do the work
  - improve the work
- Focus on process thinking
- Question and challenge existing practices, assumptions and beliefs
- Passion for, and pride in improvement
- Achieve what we want, not just fix the problem
- Active seeking and capture of ideas from any source
- A way of life - never-ending - making common sense common practice

APPENDIX B

The Operations Vision

Objectives

Quality

Element	CPA	OBJECTIVE
	Cost of Quality	To reduce the £ failure costs of quality by 30% by the end of December 1995. (Product - raw material, rework, segregate, scrap - unplanned downtime, and product and warehouse customer complaints)

Customers

Element	CPA	OBJECTIVE
	Customer Satisfaction	• To achieve a 95% despatch due date performance against lead time standards by July 1995. • To develop a measure of order accuracy by March 1995 and reduce failures to half the level recorded in Aug 1994, by Dec 1995

People

Element	CPA	OBJECTIVE
	Freedom to Act	• To achieve measurable continuing change in the level of decision making over a period of 6 months, using a decision-making matrix. • To develop understanding of empowerment down to line manager level such that a decision on the degree and rate of movement towards self-directed work teams can be made within 7 months.

Cont. Improvement

Element	CPA	OBJECTIVE
	Involvement	To have 20% of non-supervisory staff involved in CI project work by the end of July 1995, and for the project to deliver quantifiable improvements in productivity.

Performance

Element	CPA	OBJECTIVE
	Common Performance Goals	To define the first ten most important controlling or highest benefit objectives by November 1994, begin measurement and see improvement on these not later than February 1995.

Technology

Element	CPA	OBJECTIVE
	Manufacturing Costs	To achieve a 5% reduction in the manufacturing costs of foam (material, labour, energy) through technological changes to formulae and processes, measured Q4 1995 against Q4 1994.

Systems

Element	CPA	OBJECTIVE
	Ops Information Systems	To design processes and information systems which better meet user requirements, and automate these where appropriate by Sept 1995; to help to deliver inventory reduction to £3.5 million by December '95; and material spend reduction of 2% in absolute terms while supporting customer service level objectives.

APPENDIX C

Action Plan – People

Critical Performance Area:
Freedom to act

Objective:
To achieve measurable continuing change in the level of decision making over a period of 6 months, using a decision making matrix.
To develop understanding of empowerment down to line manager level such that a decision on the degree and rate of movement toward self-directed work teams can be made within 7 months.

Strategy:
Develop management understanding of the concept of self-direction through visits, study, and outside expertise. At the same time systematically increase the involvement of shop floor employees in management decision making through involvement in formal meetings and continuous improvement teams

Action Steps	Start Date	Compl Date	Resp
1. Include shop floor personnel in operational meetings and multi disciplined teams	Post workshop	30/10/94	IS/RS/ RW
2. Select training resource	19/10/94	31/1/95	IS/RS
3. Conduct attitude survey	1/11/94	31/1/95	RLS/RS
4. Develop decision-making matrix for each plant	7/11/94	31/1/95	IS/LW/ RW/AH
5. Monitor changes in level of decision making	1/2/95	30/6/95	IS/LW/ RW/AH
6. Define cultural change objectives	1/2/95	28/2/95	Ops Team
7. Educate 13 managers through training and company visits	1/3/95	1/6/95	IS/RS
8. Define the "road" to self direction	2/6/95	30/6/95	Ops Team
9. Draw up plans for progressing toward self-direction.	1/7/95	15/9/95	IS/LW/ RW/AH
10. Implement plan from step 9	1/10/95		IS/LW/ RW/AH

APPENDIX D

OPEN COLLEGE PROJECTS '95 - DUNSTABLE - 2nd PROGRESS REVIEW - 8 March 1996

Project Description	Author	Cost £'000	Benefit £'000 p.a.	Status	What Next	Sponsor
D1) In-line Mixing of Foam	John Mangan	£198	£127	Has not been pushed. Budgeted in 97. Ops Dir. wants to proceed in 96. Capex limited.	Reschedule Capex in 2nd half 96. Raise the profile of this project and get work going.	RS
D2) G2 Slitting & Packing	Sean Flanagan	£362	£91	D2 D3 & D7 combined into one project	Complete the "how to get to the objective" section of the project definition	IS
D3) Reorganise layout and material flow U11	Barry Bates	£21	£12	Objectives and action points agreed		
D7) Reduce movement Unit 11	Dave Turley	nil	Downtime £11, Safety £35	Project is running		
D4) Hot Melt working practice	Nat Rapone	?	£36 ? No baseline for measure.	D4 & D14 combined into one project. Measurement and improvement in practice is happening, but independently.	Talk to the two leaders about how to get the joint team working to maximum advantage	IS
D14) Recycle Hot Melt Adhesive.	Dave Firth	£14	£27	No teamwork between two halves of project		
D5) Export Despatch Procedure	Jackie Watson	£0.5	£6	Authorised to proceed. Awaiting Steve Bland. Export picking included in normal routine	Follow-up implementation with Steve Bland.(2-4 weeks from now)	AH
D6) Recover Waste Costs (inc. sale value of rejects & tape recovery.	Jim Furness	£13	£20	Team identified. Jim thinking about objectives. Scope of project extended to include other areas of waste	Jim to confirm objectives and "how to get there"	IS
D8) Rewind No.2 Machine	John King	£225	£157	Budgeted. Justification in progress with IG/PY.	Finalise and submit justification	RS
D9) Cell Working Foams and TT	Don Howell	?	?	Team set up. PS and 2 operators going to conf. and benchmarking visits set up.	Decide in Q2/Q3	RS
D10). Despatch Re-organisation	Sean Doyle	£11	£13	Capex approved and work complete 15/3	CLOSED	AH
D11a) Paper Accumulator	Simon Pearce	£240	£31	No action. Low pay back.	Budget in 98	RS
D11b) Utility area for Adhesive Drums	Simon Pearce	£30	£12	IBCs under consideration for adhesives	I G to progress	RS
D12) Storage & handling of foams	Ian Geldart	£65	£27	Trial jumbos this month. Work on cradle pallets Capex continues with IG	Justify cradle pallets, and continue work	RS
D13) Management of Segregate	Ray Maslin	?	?	Measure agreed. Procedure out next week	Raise the anti. Call meeting to resolve problems.	TO'B

APPENDIX E

Operations Vision: Progress review April 1995

Problem or Opportunity	Improvement Process	Resulting outputs
Multiple files for development projects	R&D Meeting	Filing restructured, only 1 file per project
Time wasted sorting out who to do what job at start of shift	Brian Betts' Team, Vision Action Plan	Nobo board for crewing written out night before
Unknown Bill of Material (BOM) accuracy leading to incorrect Standard Manufacturing Cost (SMC) and material planning	Set up audit process, check and correct. Establish control for new BOM's.	443 already checked. 86% average OK, now 100% for these. Process rolls on for remainder.
Understanding the concept of Total Quality	Housekeeping under attack	Not seen as a once every now and then - moving towards a way of life.
	Visitors tour route	More professional image to our visitors
	Move towards corporate clothing	Presents a better image. Less them and us.
	Complaints display.	Better than graphs and charts - easier to understand. Shop floor ownership.
Inconsistent cleaning of mix area	Ian Geldart's Team, Vision Action Plan	Cleaning schedule for mix area prepared and implemented
New Product Development meeting process	Structure and content being evolved to streamline meetings	Faster and more precise meetings, with much more structure
Weak development strategy and process	Strategy & R&D meetings	Process defined with gatekeepers at various stages
Delivery notes filed by Purchasing, hours of time taken per week	Ask are they needed? Talk to interested parties. Agree new process.	Now filed in weekly blocks by receiving location. Aids checking and reduces time spent.
BS 5750 : 1987 quality system	New format for procedures with flow charts	BS EN ISO 9001 : 1994 quality system with procedures re-written by those who own them
Too much high level decision making	Introduce technique of using a decision-making matrix to examine what happens and what could change.	Raise awareness, pinpoint training, plan to make changes to level of decision making. Increase level of involvement.
No training given or visible training records for technical 'A' & 'B' shifts.	Improved morale led to establishment of CI Team	Training programme for the next 12 months drawn up and skills matrix for all shift operators prepared and displayed
Ops Management Meetings boring	Team contributed ideas and suggestions for improvement	Effective communication of financial performance
	Meeting training	Presentations on improvements
	Training and structure	Good time control
Capex justification difficult and outcomes erratic		Much clearer forward plan, and high success rates on applications
Engineering/Technical Resource stretched in dealing with Capex projects.	Introduce system of Project Leader for Capex. If you want something, then you justify it.	Project leaders take ownership and involve teams (cross-functional & involving Shop Floor). Payback may be more absolute, and will be ongoing and not 'flavour of the month'.

APPENDIX F

SGB Operations Working Toward the Vision Action Plan - Systems			
Action Step	**Start**	**Compl.**	**Resp.**
1	Educate project co-ordinator	11/08/94	15/08/94	RS
2	Develop master plan and project structure	01/09/94	30/09/94	RS/
3	Educate Executive in principles of ERP	01/09/94	30/11/94	RS
4	Educate managers in concepts (11 managers x 5 days)	01/10/94	30/01/95	RS
5	Map current processes	15/11/94	Feb-95	RP
6	Identify performance measure requirements	Nov-94	Jan-95	Proj
7	Identify user requirements	Nov-94	Feb-95	RP, LW
8	Design new processes. Document policy and operating guides	Feb-95	Apr-95	Proj
9	Identify system capabilities	Jan-95	Apr-95	AH
10	Reconcile requirements and capabilities	Apr-95	Jun-95	AH
11	Applications training for users	Jun-95	Sep-95	RP
12	Conference room pilot	Aug-95	Sep-95	RS
13	Write up user guides	Sep-95	Sep-95	Use
14	Switchover	Sep-95		Team
15	Post-implementation audit	Nov-95		AH
16	Track benefits and report monthly	Sep-95	Jan-96	RP

APPENDIX G

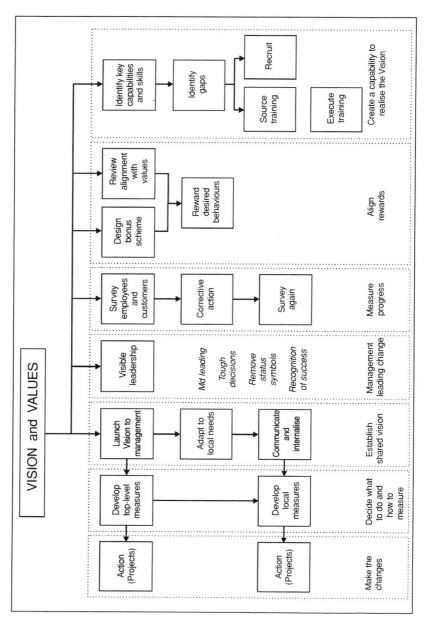

INDEX